Bedazzled!

Bedazzled!

An Astrological Guide to Earthly Bliss with Your Man

Liz Rose

THREE RIVERS PRESS • NEW YORK

Published by Three Rivers Press, New York, New York.
Member of the Crown Publishing Group, a division of Random House, Inc.
New York, Toronto, London, Sydney, Auckland
www.randomhouse.com

Printed in the United States of America

Design by Lauren Dong

Library of Congress Cataloging-in-Publication Data
Rose, Liz.
Bedazzled!:an astrological guide to earthly bliss with your man / Liz Rose.—1st ed.
p. cm.
1. Astrology. 2. Men—Psychology—Miscellanea. 3. Man-woman relationships—Miscellanea. I. Title.
BF1729 .M45 R67 2003
133.5'83067—dc21 2002155371

ISBN 1-4000-4747-1

10 9 8 7 6 5 4 3 2 1

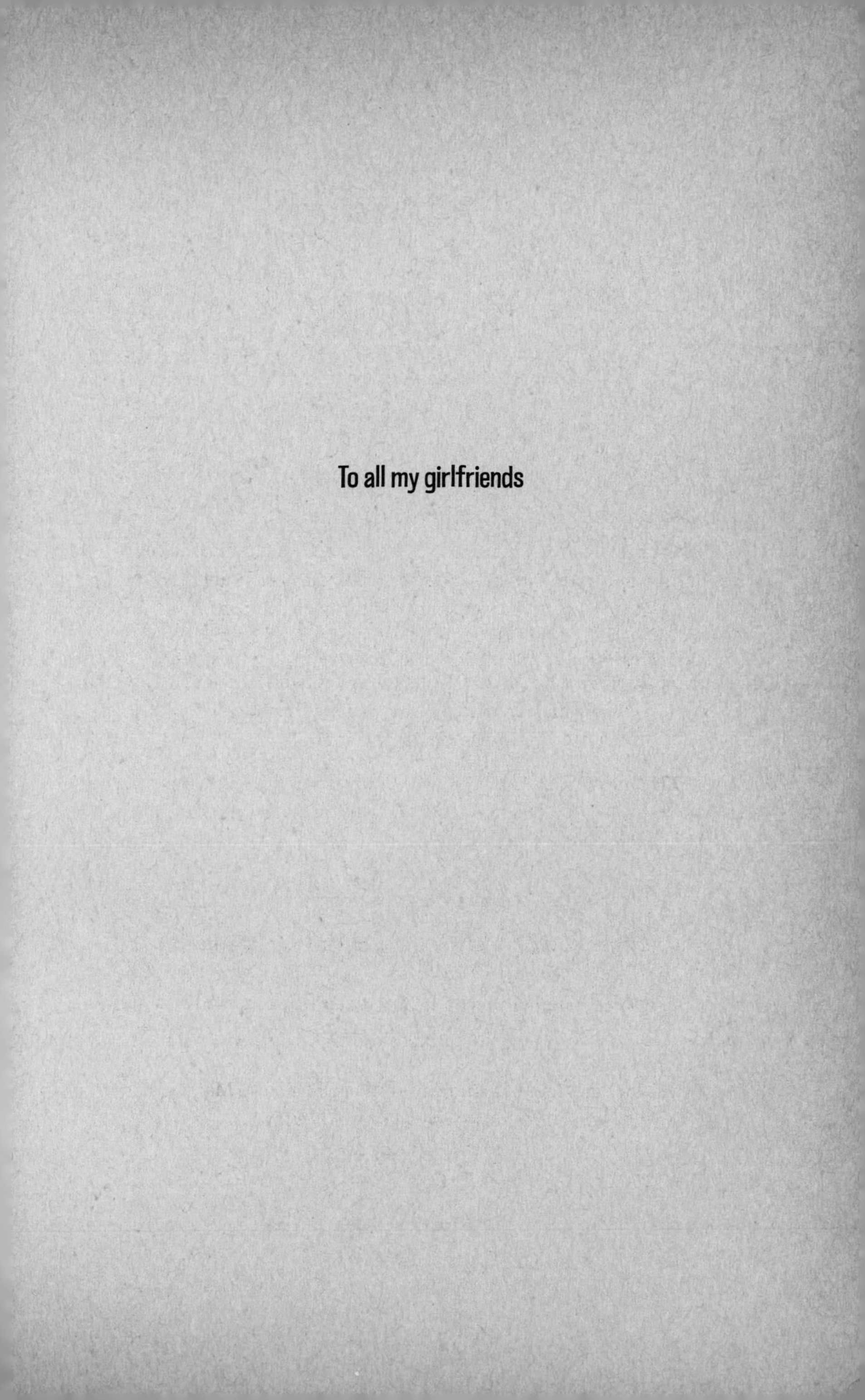

To all my girlfriends

Contents

Why I Wrote This Book

A classic scenario in my life: It's two in the morning, I'm in the middle of a great dream, and the phone rings (obviously, my Gemini friend forgets I'm in a European time zone).

Caller: *(frazzled voice)* Oh my God, Liz. You have to help me! There's this good-looking new guy in my office building. I always see him in the elevator. Anyway, I overheard him talking about some wild birthday party he had last weekend, so he must be a Sagittarius.

Me: A Sagittarius . . . Do you know what time it is?

Caller: I saw him in the lobby today. I could have sworn he winked at me. Do you think that means something? I mean, is it something he does to everyone?

Me: Probably. *(Yawn)* But that's okay for now. Do you think you'll see him again? I mean, out of the office environment?

Caller: Well, there's this new restaurant opening on Friday and I overheard he'll be there. I'm invited, too, the owners are friends of mine. How do I get his attention? What should I say?

Me: Uhhh . . . Be surrounded by some men; let him see how attractive they find you. Then, when he approaches you, and he will, be friendly but don't let him think he's God's gift to women. Play a bit, stay fun but a little sassy.

Caller: And what should I say?

Me: Let's see . . . didn't you just come back from Argentina?

Caller: Yeah, it was a disaster. Lost my luggage, got food poisoning—

Me: Well, don't mention that. Bring up your trip and make it sound like it was really unique. You can talk about some of the historical sites you visited. And it wouldn't hurt to throw in some Spanish expressions if you can remember any.

Caller: Okay. *(silence)* But why?

Me: Because Sagittarius men are fascinated by foreign countries and travel.

Caller: Should I give him my phone number if he asks?

Me: Not yet, because you'll bump into him again at work. Let it be a bit more challenging for him. Easy things bore him.

Caller: And what's the worst thing I could do?

Me: Well, if you realize you don't like him after all and you want to get rid of him, just start talking marriage and biological clocks. He'll be gone in seconds.

Caller: Hmm . . .

Me: Do you really want this guy? I mean, for a *long-term* relationship?

Caller: Maybe. That's what I want to find out.

Me: Fine. Then you'd better understand him first. Call me in the morning and we'll go over the basics. And get a good night's sleep because keeping a Sagittarius man interested will exhaust you.

Caller: Thanks, Liz! You're the greatest!

No matter that I'm an expat, living across the ocean: With the advent of the cell phone and e-mail, I'm accessible to all my single girlfriends (as well as their friends, sisters, neighbors, colleagues, etc.), who somehow think that I have nothing better to do than dole out customized dating advice! I have to be honest, I adore my girlfriends, and I really do love to be of some help, especially in important matters like dating and men. But as word spreads of my "services," a day doesn't pass when I'm not approached by one woman or another, some of whom I've never even met!

Still, I really don't mind, because I know how important relations with the opposite sex can be. Finding Mr. Right (or the closest thing to him) looms high on most women's wish list. And the journey can be a rocky road if one begins trekking with no guide or point of reference. A man's sun sign is the single best piece of information a girl can have to set her in the right direction for potential love and understanding, and now every girl can read about it (and leave me in peace!). It's about time that girls use astrology for something more than their weekly horoscope. Using the secrets of the zodiac can be the key to bedazzling the man of your dreams!

Introduction

Who ever said dating is a drag? Not a woman with the right attitude. And the right information. Getting (and keeping) a man would be easier for all women if they had an understanding of his inner workings, and the sooner the better. It's true—information really is power! And we all have the power to bedazzle a man if we're armed with the right info from the start.

But don't stress out already—getting the inside scoop on your man's basic character is easier than you think. There are no embarrassing interviews, snooping, or guessing involved—you just need to get his birth date! Knowing the astrological sun sign a man is born under gives uncanny insight into what's *really* going on in there. Sure, you've heard of astrology, but did you ever think of its capacity to empower you with the information you need in the romance department? If not, you have a fun ride ahead of you.

This guide was written for the girl who is looking for a certain kind of man or wants to bedazzle a man she has just met or already knows. And not just for one night (let's hope no gal needs advice for that), but for the long term. It's also handy for the woman who wants a realistic picture of how well she can get along with a certain guy and the long-term potential she can hope for. One girl might not want to even begin dating a man with personality traits that will annoy the hell out of her, no matter how sexy he seems today. Another one might fall in love with a certain sun sign and pray she finally bumps into a man born under it! This book will mean different things to different women, but just about everyone should get something fun and useful out of it.

To keep things simple, you only need to deal with a man's sun sign, which provides enough insight into the man you want. Besides, it's the only astrological information that's easy to get. Sure, having the entire birth chart is ideal, but how many women out there have the time or skills to make and interpret a chart for each man they meet? And how many women out there are willing to make themselves look ridiculous by demanding a man's exact time and place of birth, which is what a birth chart requires?

Using this book will help you better understand the man you want and the best way to bedazzle him. Of course, it won't always be a hundred percent correct (a sun sign is still very general), but it will definitely give you enough information to plan the best love strategy. So get busy and start reading—the dating game just got easier!

Get That Info!

"So, what's your sign?"

Pose this question on your first date and you won't be asked for a second one! The truth is, most men are suspicious of women who are into astrology. Not because they don't believe in it themselves, but because it immediately sends up a red flag. (Is this girl unstable? Weird?) This is not the way you want to begin a potential relationship!

But the *other* truth is that the answer to this notoriously stale pickup line is actually the most important piece of information a woman can have in her quest for successful dating. Still, there's absolutely no reason a man has to be made aware of this reality. Just allow your potential love interest to flounder in his ignorance while you shrewdly gather information about him that will empower you. He'll never know what hit him!

But how do you find out his sign if you cannot ask him? Well, there are dozens of clever ways for getting that info. A few ideas . . .

1. When he takes out his wallet to pay for lunch, ask if you can look at his driver's license. ("Oh, can I see your picture? It's funny how most people look nothing like themselves on ID's.")

Smile innocently while you pretend to study his photo. But store that birthday info directly into your computer brain, and don't make a mistake, because one wrong number can throw you completely off track. Excuse yourself for the ladies' room, then grab a pen and scrawl the birthday onto anything—scratch paper, a book, the palm of your hand.

2. Mention that your best friend's birthday is coming up and that you might plan a surprise party. Then you can ask if he's ever been given a surprise birthday party. If he says no, you can say something like, "Oh, were you one of those people who had a summer birthday, when everyone was on vacation?" He might say yes, and since you're already on the subject, you can ask, "When?" He'll give you the date, then you can utter that your cousin has the same birthday and then *quickly* move on to a new subject. Now, if he answered no to your question, you can casually ask when it is. As long as you are on the topic of birthdays, he should not get suspicious.

3. If none of this works, you could just ask him his birthday (but not while you're on a romantic date). Just say your best guy friend in high school looks and acts exactly like him and it'd be interesting to see if he has the same birthday.

If you try any of the above methods (or one of your own inventions) and the guy immediately asks if you are "into" astrology, *deny it* at all costs! "What? I don't even know what sign I am." Something like that.

It's true you might meet a guy who is actually fascinated by astrology (there are probably more than you think) and who would delight in sharing his pertinent information. Still, it's best to keep a low profile until you really get to know him.

Now What?

Finally, you have the magical date! The next thing to do is see which sun sign it falls under (the dates are listed in each chapter). Just be careful of the first or last date of each sun sign—either might be off by one day. The fact is that a sun sign never begins at the exact same moment each year. One year, the sign of Taurus might begin at 9:20 P.M. on April 19, and the next year at 5:16 A.M. on April 20. Unless you have the exact time and place of birth and a special computer program or an ephemeris (okay, this is getting too technical), you cannot know for sure.

Still, two adjacent signs are so different from each other that you should be able to tell which one your guy falls into. Observe the man, listen to how he talks, listen to what he says, look at how he dresses, how he holds himself, how he chooses to spend his free time, etc. It just takes a little intuition to know which of the two signs he is and which one he definitely is not. When you're sure you know your man's sun sign, just find the appropriate chapter and read on.

By the way, some people born on the last days of a sun sign display its characteristics less strongly than those people whose birthdays fall at the very beginning of a sign, when its "energy" is at its most pure. Probably the reason is that the last days of a particular sign begin to lose their power as they ready themselves for the induction of the following one. These people born at the end of a cusp might draw in some personality traits of the next sign, so their character ends up being more of a blend of two signs. Still, there's really no absolute rule. A man born on the last day of Leo can appear even more "leonine" than a man born on the first day, so you never know.

When Opposites Attract

It's true that some men are attracted to women who are fundamentally the opposite of themselves. Maybe this attraction exists because there are things about their own character that they don't like (or even hate). Or maybe they seek someone who will complement, rather than exaggerate, their own qualities. Maybe they are just looking for a woman who will help bring out another dimension in themselves. And sometimes they find her.

Then there are always the guys who are excited by "difficult" girls, ones who cause friction, or ones who present a bigger challenge because they're so different and hard to figure out. Unfortunately, this dynamic scenario often fizzles out after the infatuation period, especially when these two people have absolutely nothing in common (though it can lead to better self-understanding for both parties). As in *Gone With the Wind,* Ashley Wilkes would have loved to bed Scarlett, but he *wed* Melanie. Big difference.

As you read this book, you'll learn how each sun sign coupling is rated ("Best Bets," "Why Not?," and "Challenging") based on the potential for a long-term relationship (and not a spring fling or a fatal attraction). The prevailing logic is that an enduring and successful relationship works best when there is mutual understanding and similar attitudes between two people, so the best matches are between signs that have at least *something* in common. (But not necessarily *too much* in common, as is the case with same-sign pairings, which often lack dimension or are "too much of a good thing.") Still, "challenging" combinations of signs can work together . . . but it will be *work* a lot of the time. If you're patient and flexible enough to make the appropriate compromises, maybe you should give it a try. Whatever happens, it could be more interesting than a relationship with no sparks.

Anyway, the compatibility rating is just a general indication of the love potential for two signs. What's clearly more important is how you personally feel about the general character of a particular man and how well you can get along with him, *regardless of your own sign.* If you can only love a certain kind of man, then maybe he's meant for you, even if you are supposedly incompatible. (Ideally, you can be objective about the true potential between you.) You know better than anyone else who is right and wrong for you, so let your intuition guide you when in doubt.

Who Are You, Anyway?

Included in each sun sign chapter is some enlightening info on what behavior works and doesn't work ("Dos and Don'ts") with the men of that sun sign. There's also a handy fashion section that not only describes a man's general preferences for female fashion, but gives insight into his attitude toward clothes and shopping, which for some girls out there are major life issues. Again, it's all info you can use to your advantage, and even if you choose not to make sweeping changes in your own comportment to bedazzle a certain man, at least you'll get a better idea of where he's coming from. *(So that's why he hates to kiss in public!)* Maybe more important is the realization that a certain guy is simply not for you. Why waste time on a man who could never appreciate the type of woman you are?

Then again, what "type" of woman are you, really? Isn't it possible there may be hidden facets of your personality that have yet to be drawn out? It seems that most women are much more complex than they realize. A girl who always thought of herself as adventuresome and independent might really crave stability and guidance deep down inside. Or another, who was resigned to her fate as the modest librarian type, might discover that she does, indeed, have a latent glamorous streak that is dying to get out. The inspiring truth is that different men can draw out different aspects of ourselves, ones we never expressed or even acknowledged—it's really fascinating. And the benefit in staying open to exploring the different kinds of women you can be is that you might discover things about yourself you were not even aware of. You might even become a happier person for it. So have fun and experiment with different looks and "personalities" if you feel like it—you might have some big surprises in store for you! (And that doesn't exclude appealing to a much wider group of men out there.)

Still, as you're brushing up on your table etiquette for the new Capricorn man in your life, never forget about the magical nature of love. To this day, nobody has come up with the secret recipe for love, even though we all know that a certain chemistry just *has* to be there. Knowing a man and the kind of woman he likes cannot "invent" chemistry and magic—it can only steer one in the right direction for potential love and understanding. But that's already a notable step.

A Little Technical Stuff

Most men reflect their sun signs, but there will be a few who don't seem to fit it at all. This may happen when their rising sign is fundamentally different from their sun sign (for example, a man with a Taurus sun sign and Aquarius rising sign), or when they have a bunch of planets in another sign (a man with a Taurus sun sign and five planets in Gemini). Now, this may already be getting too technical for you, but the point to remember is that many factors come into play that can modify the sun sign. (See "Quick and Easy Explanations," below.)

If you *really* want to know a guy well, it would help to know his rising and moon signs. For whatever reason you happen to fall upon this information, study the corresponding chapters and incorporate these signs into his sun sign.

For example, take a man with a Taurus sun sign, Virgo moon sign, and Aquarius rising sign. He will still be a Taurus and therefore be fond of stability, money, affection, and good living, but his Virgo moon may add a critical and analytical element to his emotions, and his Aquarius rising will color his typically conservative Taurus nature with more individuality and eccentricity.

Okay, this might already sound confusing to some, so be happy to know that the sun sign is all you need to understand the broad strokes of a man. In time, you'll discover the other hidden parts of him that a natal chart might have pointed out. And hands-on experience is always more fun than textbook learning!

QUICK AND EASY EXPLANATIONS

Rising sign (ascendant) = Zodiacal sign that is on the Eastern horizon the moment one is born. Colors and individualizes the sun sign. Determined by the exact time and place of birth.

Moon sign = Zodiacal sign of the moon at exact time and place of birth. Changes about every two and a half days. Sheds light on one's emotional makeup.

Other planets = Mercury, Venus, Mars, Jupiter, Saturn, Uranus, Neptune, and Pluto (as of today). Each planet is located in a zodiacal sign at any given moment. Depending on time and place of birth, each planet influences character, some more than others.

To Whom It May Concern

For those of you who may have read other books on astrology, you will notice some differences of opinion in this one. For example, most books insist that all air signs—that is, Gemini, Libra, and Aquarius—fit well together. True, they may fit well together on the intellectual level, or on the social level, but that doesn't mean they work well together in the love arena. An Aquarian lives for independence and change. A Libran strives for equilibrium and partnership. How could a long-term love relationship thrive between a dependent Libra man and a freedom-seeking Aquarius woman? It might work in the beginning, but the basic differences in their needs could very well present future obstacles.

Just the same, you might wonder why some signs you had been told were incompatible get positive treatment in this book. It's because their "differences" actually work well together, and one of their few similarities provides enough common ground to make for a potentially strong couple.

In this book, the couple's compatibility rating reflects the true potential of certain love combinations, as opposed to nice and neat formulas that seem to work out perfectly in other books. It's as simple as that.

Unusual Forms of Sun Signs

Strangely enough, some men manifest characteristics of a sun sign in one of its rarer forms. Usually what happens is that one of a sun sign's positive or negative qualities is played out to an extreme (e.g., Taurus greed to an extreme can result in the deviant form of Taurus called "The Bulldozer"). In other instances, a man just becomes a "derivative" of a sun sign—he starts out as the essence of the sun sign, then somewhere along the way, he inexplicably mutates into a more unusual form. Still, the man is usually true to his sun-sign fundamentals deep down.

Then you might meet a guy who totally resembles his sun sign, yet surprises you from time to time with exaggerated behavior in sync with one of the sun sign's more rare forms. Don't worry, it can happen, but it's usually quite temporary and infrequent.

Most men will reflect the basics of their sun signs, so that's all you really have to know. But if you're dying to know what other kinds of men are lurking out there and what else you might encounter, check out the appendix at the end of the book.

Aries, the Ram

(about March 21 till about April 20)

Make no mistake about it, girls: The Aries man is the Real Male, equipped mentally and physically to win in both love and war. Like the horned Ram, he charges mightily toward the object of his desire and won't stop until he has won. The bigger the challenge, the greater the glory, so obstacles are not only accepted but welcomed.

It's hard to resist the Aries man (unless you happen to like weak ones); no other creature can make a woman *really* feel like a woman. When he wants you, he will do everything to have you, even if it means stealing you from another man—including fiancés and husbands! No, he's not selfish (well, maybe) or mean (certainly not). The simple truth is that a Ram can be blinded by passion to the point where good judgment and the question of ethics are forgotten. But let's be honest. Isn't it darned romantic? Is there any girl out there who could hate a guy who would duel for her? This is the guy who would die fighting for you, making him an imminent threat for men of the meeker sort. And, needless to say, the Ram usually wins the battle.

The Aries man is direct. He has no patience for beating around the bush, because time is of the essence and he has things to accomplish. This is generally good for the girl who needs to know exactly where she stands in a relationship (though more complex gals might find this approach too simple). No, this is not the guy to play around with a girl's heart. He's sincere and has no time for games.

The Ram has dreamt about his ideal woman since he was young and often goes through many girls before finding one who comes even close to his dream. He falls in "love" with lightning speed, convinced he has finally found the one he's been searching for, only to be disappointed later when he discovers she does not live up to his ideal. This is why the Aries man can account for many more infatuations than true loves. Still, there is a girl out there for him. She just has to make him realize it.

In general, he tends to fall for very feminine women, like the long-haired fair maiden, because he still believes in traditional roles: the strong male, the soft female. This is why he runs away from strong, pushy women. Remember, *he* is the hunter, not the prey, and will cool off the minute he feels chased by a woman. However, the female of a more gentle breed often ends up being too submissive and easy, and it's not long before the Aries man tires of her and is off on a more challenging quest. The best woman for him is one who can find the right balance of yin and yang—she should have force underneath her vulnerable facade, and never make him a hundred percent sure she's been "conquered." That's the only way to keep his desire flowing, which is the key to holding the Ram's interest in the long term.

To tell you the truth, this is the guy who probably has a subscription to the Victoria's Secret catalog and fantasizes about sleeping with Laetitia Casta. Fortunately, though, he realizes that she and her colleagues are out of even his far-reaching grasp and he'll bring his own aspirations down to earth. Still, it's clear that physical attraction is a top priority for this man. A girl can be brilliant, funny, rich, whatever, but if she elicits no sexual sparks and no desire to bed her, the Ram will want her only as a friend he can confide his true crushes to. Still, the Aries man makes a great friend. You might not get him in bed, but at least you can share in a warm and dynamic friendship.

If physical beauty is not one of your strengths, you can learn to make the most of what you do have. Flaunt your best assets, hide your worst ones. Try to cultivate your sex appeal (which is unrelated to beauty) with provocative body language, flirty eyes, a charming smile. Learn how to make men notice you when you walk into a room. *Believe* you have sexual power and your Aries man will start to believe it, too.

The Ram is also impressed with success, as long as it's not markedly greater than his own. Do well at your job, flaunt your promotions, have lots of friends, and attend many parties. Try to "shine" in whatever you are good at and this man might take notice.

Most of all, the Ram is obsessed with virility and youth (which is why he may engage in sports and activities typically suited for big boys). So don't let yourself "age" mentally or physically at a rapid pace. Likewise, never make the mistake of making your Aries lover feel old or "over the hill" (you'd kill him).

Whatever specific qualities the Ram looks for in a woman, she must be desirable, not only to him, but to his friends, his enemies, and just about everyone else. It's amazing to see how quickly an Aries man can change his assessment of a girl based on what other men think. If every other man wants a girl he overlooked, she must be a prize after all—this is his logic. It cannot be underestimated how important it is that other people find his girlfriend attractive, because, in the end, the Aries man is really seeking glory.

Just make sure you're never his "rebound" girl. After a disillusioning relationship, especially if he is dumped by a girl he thinks he loves (very rare, but it happens), an embittered Aries man can seek demeaning or promiscuous relationships with women he cares nothing for. You'll know it by the look in his eyes. When he's falling in love, his eyes sparkle. When he's on the rebound, his eyes harden. Fortunately, though, the Ram's enthusiasm usually wins out in the end and enables him to pursue his dreams again.

So if your heart has been conquered by an Aries male, be in for an exciting and passionate relationship, as well as difficult moments and occasional scenes. The Aries man expects exclusive love and won't take an innocent flirt with another man too well. At the same time, he's impressed when other men covet his girl. Nothing can make his heart skip faster than entering a room and knowing every set of male eyes is on his girlfriend. Just don't make the mistake of responding to the attention, however subtle. Your eyes are meant only for your Aries lover.

THE ARIES MAN IS

AT BEST	AT WORST
Energetic	Egocentric
Assertive	Belligerent
Passionate	Naive
Adventurous	Selfish
Pioneering	Reckless
Enterprising	Aggressive
Ambitious	Exhausting
Dynamic	Macho
Enthusiastic	Impatient
Confident	Headstrong
Self-Motivated	Irritable
Ardent	Uncooperative
Competitive	Accident-Prone
Courageous	Undiplomatic
Direct	Rude

He might also expect you to make his agenda top priority. For him, it's a question of principle. He fought for you, he's the man in the relationship, simple as that (try not to laugh). This is a problem for the modern woman, but not an insolvable one. Just let him believe that his interests are first, and he won't even question it afterward. (He's a bit naive and easy to fool, by the way.) The Ram has so many virtues that you'll have to forgive his medieval thinking.

When the fire is burning, this ardent man will make you forget all the others. And you could fall so in love that you lose your head with him. Just don't let that flame burn out! To make it past the infatuation stage, you'll have to walk on a tightrope, between strength and vulnerability, independence and submissiveness. Keep your relationship lively, dynamic, and challenging, whatever it takes. And always be a woman.

SOME FAMOUS ARIES MEN

Russell Crowe, Warren Beatty, Hugh Hefner, Dennis Quaid, Eddie Murphy, Eric Clapton, Alec Baldwin, Steve McQueen, Howard Cosell, Gregory Peck, Francis Ford Coppola, Omar Sharif, Al Gore, Christopher Walken, David Letterman, Marlon Brando, Thomas Jefferson, Casanova, Robert Downey Jr., Quentin Tarantino

MUST HAVE BEEN AN ARIES MAN

Rhett Butler *(Gone With the Wind)*

THE SEDUCTION

This direct man doesn't have the time or imagination to scheme up an Academy Award–deserving seduction. It's often (too) simple, as in Boy Meets Girl, Boy Wants Girl, Boy Conquers Girl, so don't be put off by his rudimentary tactics if you're one of those more complicated women. He's a man, you're a woman, you belong together, it's as simple as that.

If you know him through school or work, it's no coincidence when he happens to be heading down the same hallway as you. This animal knows your basic routine and incorporates himself into it, just to get closer and make the next move. If you live on the other side of town, or even in the boondocks, no problem.

A real Aries man will go any distance for a girl he must have, convinced she is worth the effort. In any case, the Ram will get down to the essentials quickly and never leave you in doubt about his desires. You'll entice him even more by acting a bit coy.

When he asks you out, don't be too available, especially in the beginning. You don't want him to think you don't have plans for Friday night (or any night, for that matter). And while he's busy encircling you in the coming weeks (days), raise the stakes by letting him see how many other guys find you utterly attractive. Of course, you don't want to play too much, or expect him to beg. But never be too easy or eager.

When you finally do go on a first date, make sure it's a big success. But that doesn't mean he needs to score! On the contrary, he must want you even more than before. Yes, you can kiss and see how well you "connect" on the lip level. But don't let this sexy man conquer you right away, no matter how hard it is to resist him (and sometimes it's pretty damn hard!). Do not make the mistake of thinking that you are an "exception" to the rule. Sure, he might make you feel like the only woman on earth, that you are truly "the one," but that's because he hasn't had you yet.

As you begin to date, you'll have to give in to his manhood, but do it slowly and deliciously, leaving him always wanting more. Let yourself be conquered, little by little, but without appearing too weak. And when you finally do decide to go all the way, make sure you are prepared—that means a perfectly smooth body, soft skin, light body scent, and flirty lingerie. The first time must be *great* and make him feel like a stud. If your first sexual experience even remotely resembles a failure, don't bother waiting for his phone call or the next date—it's *over,* girl!

After your first time in bed, be honest with yourself about the chemistry. If there doesn't seem to be mutual passion already, don't go thinking long term, because it won't last. But if you seem to be made for each other, make your Ram feel that he's the *best* lover in the world, and that you have never known better. (A little white lie is not a crime!)

SEX

ardent, passionate, quick, frequent

Sex makes the world go round. Or at least that's what your Ram thinks. Yes, he enjoys sex more than most other men out there, but not only because of the physical satisfaction he derives; he loves sex because it's the easiest (and most fun) way of proving his manhood and virility and ensuring that, were it up to his macho self, the human species would indeed continue.

Because he's often seized in a moment of passion, sex with him can be a bit, uh, rushed—sometimes over before you count to twenty! He'll never admit it, but one wonders if he really doesn't believe that men should enjoy it more. Then, what's ironic is that he expects it to be an amazing and fulfilling experience for you, and if you let him feel that it was anything less than heroic, he could zip up and take his equipment elsewhere.

If he's a bit older, maybe he's already learned to slow down (or maybe an ex-girlfriend cruelly informed him of his poor endurance). If not, try introducing some delay tactics—prolong the flirting, the kissing, the caressing. But never criticize him—quick sex is better than no sex.

As for the sex itself, stay on the clean side. True, he does enjoy some hard-core sex with girls he has no emotional ties to, but if you want to be his girlfriend, aim for enjoyable, passionate sex that stays within the boundaries of decency. Sometimes the Ram crudely divides females into two groups—those meant for flings and those meant for love. If you're aiming for the second category, enjoy great sex, but never get raunchy. If you do, he might show some approval at first, but after a while, he could lose respect for you and seek more "pure" loving elsewhere.

DOS AND DON'TS OF A GREAT RELATIONSHIP

DO

Showcase your feminine nature and assets.
Be stimulating, physically and intellectually.
Know how to be an effective flirt (but only for him!).
Be romantic and passionate and sexy, all at once.
Make sure he notices how attractive other men find you.
Put him on a pedestal (but don't let it go to his head).
Enjoy spontaneity and last-minute plans.
Be difficult from time to time.
Make him feel like a man.
Give him praise for his feats and achievements.
Stay *young* in mind and body.
Encourage his latest plans or dreams (unless they're completely silly).
Let him see the high self-esteem you have for yourself.
Win brownie points with his male friends.
Let him know how attractive he is.

DON'T

Be too strong or bossy.
Be slow or boring.
Come off as frigid or cold.
Be pessimistic and critical.
Be weak and too easy.
Flirt obnoxiously with other men.
Play games too long.
Lie or beat around the bush.
Bruise his great ego.
Injure his virility or manhood.
Insist that you're right all the time.
Lose your sex appeal.
Give in all the time.
Pick unnecessary fights.

BEST WAYS TO IMPRESS

Be a top model or the winner of a beauty pageant.
Be an "It-girl."
Be a young entrepreneur.
Make a magazine cover (for whatever admirable reason).
Be a virgin with an endless line of admirers.

BEST WAYS TO GET DUMPED

Sleep with his boss, then flaunt what a better lover he is.
Side with one of his rivals.
Be voted "the most unattractive girl" by his group of buddies.
Dress like a nun.
Pamper your dog more than him.

FASHION

This macho guy likes the real female, regardless of the current trends. Even when the "androgynous" look is all the rage, the Ram will give short shrift to a woman in asexual clothing, so ignore fashion's more unreasonable moments and dress for your Ram. Like a real man, he'll have no idea if you're wearing a Prada dress, anyway, so don't waste your money on such pricey threads. All that matters is how the dress fits and how appealing it makes you look. By the way, avoid too much black, which can add a harsh edge, and go for some pastels, whites, or even a red.

Youthful, feminine clothes work the best, especially those that showcase your best asset and elicit admiration without being vulgar. Another winning look is the innocent/sexy combination, one that draws out a sort of *vulnerable sexiness* that the Ram is a total sucker for. Anyway, you'll know if you're wearing the right outfit by observing his very first reaction upon seeing you—if he's delighted, his face will light up, but if he's disappointed, he'll have to force a smile. (And sometimes he'll even become grumpy.)

Accessories are welcome but not really necessary. And too much jewelry looks "old." But extras like feminine earrings or sexy open-toed heels always work. So does beautiful lingerie. Still, no accessory could be more important than soft, silky skin, so keep things simple by focusing on your face and body regimen. And keep the tresses down. It's not that difficult to look *irrestible.*

GIFT IDEAS: Those that are personal or exclusive.

BEER BUDGET

Personalized music mix on cassette or CD
Two tickets to his favorite sporting event
Book about one of his hobbies
Manly cologne
Workout clothes
Sporty shirt (his favorite color)

CHAMPAGNE BUDGET

Monogrammed anything
"Success" briefcase
Membership to great gym
Custom-made suit
Big-screen TV
Sports car

ADD SOME SPICE

Don't let your relationship become old and stale. Throw in some spice regularly (but don't go overboard).

Some Ideas

1. Compete in a game or sport you know you'll beat him in, then "give in" when he seduces you to prove his manhood.
2. Get into some kind of trouble, then let him "rescue" you heroically.
3. Just when he's beginning to think you can't function without him anymore, surprise him with some daringly independent behavior.
4. Let your eyes linger, just fleetingly, on a handsome stranger.

IF YOU SENSE A LOOMING BREAKUP

You won't have to guess your Aries man's intentions if he plans to leave you, because his actions are so direct and genuine. And what was a great relationship last week could be a tiresome one this week, so things evolve quite rapidly, for the good or the bad. If you have enough time to sense trouble, though, act *quickly* before it's too late.

Danger Signs to Watch For

- Growing or sudden boredom
- Lower irritation threshold
- Fewer phone calls and less attention
- Increasing and obvious interest in other females
- Just a general "cooling down"

If you're still crazy about him and want to redeem yourself before he breaks the bad news, date another man, and fast! The Aries man relishes the challenge of winning back his ex, despite the reasons for the burnout (he probably forgot them already). Be difficult, almost impossible, then give him a second chance if you want him (but never a third).

You could also turn the tables and make it look like it's *you* who wants to move on. Cancel a date (without any good explanation), lessen the eye contact, be a bit more open to the attention of other men. This *un*intuitive man needs concrete actions to enlighten him, so forget about using double wordplay or implicit statements to get your message across—you have to hit him over the head with it.

And if, despite everything, he still breaks it off, know that it's only positively over *for now.* You wouldn't believe it, but this Ram is actually a sentimental guy at heart and holds a torch for his more beloved ex-flames. Even if he's absorbed in a new love, he'll always be interested to hear the whereabouts of an ex. (Hearing she's engaged to Mr. Super Stud or was named Female of the Year immediately propels her back into the *Desirable* category!) So if he breaks up with you, accept that it's *over* (for now) and just kind of disappear from his life—that means no drunken late-night phone calls, nostalgic sex, or "buddy" dates. And to make him really regret his mistake, get on with your life, date some incredible men, and (this will kill him) let him believe it was easy to forget him.

AND NEVER FORGET

His essential need to prove his manhood

HOW MR. ARIES SEES YOU

	AT BEST	AT WORST
Aries	dynamic, passionate	competitive, masculine
Taurus	feminine, sensual	slow, boring
Gemini	youthful, fun	androgynous, cerebral
Cancer	feminine, supple	moody, fickle
Leo	bright, passionate	strong, domineering
Virgo	kind, intelligent	critical, modest

Libra	feminine, accommodating	conciliatory, easy
Scorpio	sexy, magnetic	manipulative, controlling
Sagittarius	fun, daring	tomboyish, negligent
Capricorn	ambitious, loyal	old, harsh
Aquarius	intriguing, challenging	independent, aloof
Pisces	feminine, romantic	weak, dishonest

COUPLES COMPATIBILITY

BEST BETS	WHY NOT?	CHALLENGING
Gemini	Taurus	Cancer
Leo	Scorpio	Capricorn
Aquarius	Virgo	
Libra	Aries	
	Sagittarius	
	Pisces	

ARIES MAN (Warren Beatty) and GEMINI WOMAN (Annette Bening)

A dynamic duo! Neither sign is known for endurance in the love department, but they could go a long way when they team up together. We all know the Aries man loves women. Lots of them. And unless he finds the right one, he can end up a perennial bachelor, always in search of a new prize. Bumping into a Gemini woman might stop him in his tracks, because if there's one woman who can intrigue him for longer than a month, it's Ms. Gemini. This is the gal who can make the Aries man feel *young,* with her flirty smile, quick wit, and sometimes juvenile behavior. And because she usually maintains a youthful mind and figure throughout life, she'll never drag him down by seeming "old." To top it off, the Gemini gal is clever enough to see that her Aries man is *never* bored. Just leave it to her to find new ways of stimulating him, challenging him, and turning him on. It might take lots of tricks to keep him interested, but if there's one woman who can rise to the challenge, this is who it is. On her side, Ms. Gemini will appreciate the Aries man's energy and virility. And she'd be lucky if he could teach her the difference between words and *action.*

SOME ADVICE—TAKE IT OR LEAVE IT

YOUR SIGN	
Aries	DO: remember you are still a woman DON'T: compete and try to be stronger
Taurus	DO: exaggerate your feminine allure DON'T: get too settled too quickly
Gemini	DO: indulge in fun and flirt DON'T: disappoint him with your easy lies
Cancer	DO: entice him with your ultra-femininity DON'T: sap his energy with your dark brooding
Leo	DO: play up your endearing sense of loyalty DON'T: boss him around and make him feel small
Virgo	DO: accentuate the "virgin" in you DON'T: let your self-control seem like lack of interest
Libra	DO: delight him with your charm and femininity DON'T: be totally easy and unchallenging
Scorpio	DO: be sexy without being overtly sexual DON'T: let your relationship become all about sex
Sagittarius	DO: work on cultivating a feminine mystique DON'T: be careless about love and romance
Capricorn	DO: fuel his ambition by helping him set long-term goals DON'T: be too serious and stifle his enthusiasm
Aquarius	DO: intrigue him with your fresh and unique allure DON'T: cool him off with your impersonal touches
Pisces	DO: enchant him with your romantic view of love DON'T: be weak, suffering, and (especially) dishonest in love

Looking Farther Down the Road

THE ENGAGEMENT

The Ram could pop the question as quickly as he could dump you. This is one man who could end a whirlwind romance with a sudden proposal if he's convinced you're the "one"—the more he prizes you, the quicker he'll make the next move. On the other hand, because he's one of the faster-moving animals around, he's not the type to let a futureless relationship drag on for long.

If he's not sure about you, or if's he's just with you for sex, he may stay with you only until something better pops up. So figure him out early. If you're sure he's on the "lookout," send him a clear message by enjoying the attention of a formidable competitor. And if you want to do something more risky, consider "tiring" of him and moving on to your next beau. Don't worry, if he really wants you, he'll woo you back in no time, and this time he might offer you a ring. On the other hand, if he seems without regret, be glad to have cut your losses and moved on.

THE WEDDING

Start making wedding plans as soon as possible, even if it's just behind the scenes. And continue to maintain a romantic relationship with your fiancé throughout the engagement period. This is a precarious time—there are all sorts of (female) threats out there that could make your engagement null and void, so it's crucial you dazzle your Ram right up until the wedding day. Never take him for granted just because you have a ring.

This day must be victorious, so plan well and allow for *no* blunders. And don't even think about sneaking some ex-beaus onto the guest list—your Aries man should be the center of your universe. This is his day, too, after all. Of course, he'll want all the male invites to covet the woman he's about to marry, so make sure to wow him with your unprecedented beauty as you walk down the aisle. Just be careful about the females you choose as bridesmaids—you wouldn't want them to challenge you in the desirability department.

THE HONEYMOON

The Aries man will be enthusiastic to race off to a romantic holiday, so try to be as excited as he is. And don't ever let this trip get boring! Wherever you go, make sure there are lots of things to do. True, the sex will be high priority, but there are twenty-four hours in a day. It'd be a good idea to incorporate some sporting activities into your agenda, too, since the Ram can get very grouchy if he begins to feel flabby. At least try to locate a gym if there's no other way to burn off fat. This is your dream vacation, and your Ram won't feel studly if he gets a beer belly.

Just don't make the trip too long. Since the Aries man tires quickly, it's better to plan a shorter, more intense honeymoon than a long one that drags on forever. In fact, the best moment to end it is when it is at its peak; that way, you can savor the memories of an intensely happy trip rather than one that began to fizzle out. But if you really want a month with your sweetheart, think about hopping to several destinations so that your trip stays fresh and exciting.

Honeymoon Sex

The first post-wedding encounter should be lovely. Since the Aries man has the tendency to like everything fresh and new, you might want to play the born-again virgin, with a brand-new white baby-doll negligee and matching panties, a lot of flirting, and some coy behavior. Make him feel like a boy again, let yourself feel "shiny and new," make it feel like the very first time.

MAKING IT IN THE LONG HAUL

Because the future (and past) is of less interest to the Aries man than the present moment, this is not someone who will put all his energy into creating something that will be beautiful twenty years from now. That includes relationships and includes marriage. And you should never begin taking your Aries husband for granted—he has no qualms about ending a marriage when he doesn't feel appreciated. Besides, the notion of starting a fresh new life with someone else will always loom high on his secret wish list, so don't give him a good excuse to pack up. Once you're past the idealistic newlywed phase, it will be up to you to find ways to keep the marriage dynamic and fresh.

DOS AND DON'TS FOR LASTING BLISS

DO

Renew yourself by taking up new hobbies and interests.

Change your look from time to time (unless he just loves the way you are).

Stay fit with sports or the gym.

Keep a busy agenda (restaurants, parties, sports, etc.).

Continue to make him feel attractive.
Let him look (just look) at pretty females.
Be open to change (of house, career, etc.) if he really needs it.
Continue to encourage him on his chosen path.
Know how to sense his burnout periods and help him to find new energy.
Let him blow off his steam when he needs to.
Help make his dreams come true.
Do your best to stay attractive and desirable.
Challenge him from time to time.
Make him feel attractive and sexy.
Let him notice, regularly, that other men still find you attractive.

Take him (or your marriage) for granted—-ever.
Let him take you (or your marriage) for granted.
Let him make *all* the decisions.
Invite young beautiful women into your home.
Slip into a boring, daily routine, void of spontaneity and energy.
Try to become the big boss now that you're legally bound.
Unnecessarily reveal your flaws.
Do everything he says or become his slave.
Stifle his enthusiasm or mock his latest plans.
Withhold sex to punish him (he'll just seek it elsewhere).
Make him feel old (even when he's eighty).
Let yourself become a lazy couch potato.
Lose that sparkle in your eye.
Become a nag and whine about every little thing.
Become blasé and burnt-out on life.
Chop off your long tresses (but if you *must* make the cut, keep it girlish and natural—think Meg Ryan).

EARTHLY BLISS (AKA SEX)

How many times do you want to hear it? Keep the sex great! More than any other man, your Aries husband needs amazing sex to convince him of his virility and manhood, and as he ages, it may become an even higher priority. There is nothing more defeating than an Aries man (even a father or grandfather) who is made to feel that he just can't perform anymore. So what if he's really not up to par? Your Aries man must never know it!

To keep it fun in the long run, you will probably have to find new positions and places, but decent ones, and nothing vulgar or "hard" (that kind of sex is suited for prostitutes, not his dear wife). Nothing weird, either. (No, you won't excite him by hanging naked, upside down, from your gym equipment.) Your Aries man wants to think of you as the fresh girl he seduced many years ago, so keep it fun, romantic, and rewarding. And don't ever let the sex become a "given." Sex to the enamored Aries man should be the reward of winning over the heart of his girl, the ultimate prize. So let him continue to woo you. And keep up the pre-sex seductions—the flirting, the feminine wiles, the whole shebang—even ten years down the road. Sure, you'll have to change your tactics regularly, but keep the road to sex inspiring and passionate and make him win you over each time.

If you find yourself growing tired as you get older, don't show it! Think about dropping one of your time-consuming and unnecessary activities so you are fresh when your Aries man needs some loving. And never make the mistake of making him feel undesirable. This is critical to a lasting relationship. At the same time, though, you shouldn't *always* give in when he wants it—otherwise you become a "given." If you resist, invent a good reason (like he hasn't been sweet enough to you lately, or you're still upset that he was rude to your mother, etc.). Not only will it get him to think about his selfish actions, it will make his desire for you build until the next time he can win you over.

AND CHEATING . . . ?

Yes, you know he hungers for sweet young things. But will he actually cheat on you? You'll hate to hear it, but it's definitely possible! Especially in the long run, when you start to get arthritis and other symptoms of old age. If you're quite a bit younger than him (or at least look and act like it), there may be fewer potential problems. But a woman who ages at the same rate as her Aries man (or faster) will feel the heat in the coming years.

The biggest danger point may be when the Aries man undergoes his midlife crisis. Strange ideas enter his head as he begins to question his marriage and life. Worse for him is the subtle understanding that he is in the final stage of what he considers "youth." If he feels locked inside a boring and loveless marriage, he might think about making a break and starting all over again.

Once the Aries man feels he's lost his power (at whatever age that may be), he usually mellows out and gives up on his dreams of fresh love and new babes. Besides, he doesn't particularly relish the idea of being out in the arena competing with virile thirty-five-year-olds. But if he maintains his sex appeal and thinks he's still "got it," even at sixty-five, nothing is out of his reach.

Still, although the Ram loves to look and fantasize, his idealistic and romantic nature doesn't lend itself well to sad endings. He wants a fairy tale, and fairy tales have happy endings. If his princess can keep the relationship exciting, dynamic, and fresh, and if she can make her Aries husband feel attractive and outstanding, she should be able to keep him in the long run.

REASONS HE MIGHT CHEAT

- If he's thirsting for the intoxicating rush of new love
- If he wants to feel young again
- If he needs to "compete" with another friend who just conquered a young beauty
- If you've let your marriage become old or dead
- If you make him feel undesirable and old

WHAT YOU CAN DO

- Invest in *lots* of lingerie.
- Plan many short romantic getaways.
- Make him feel handsome and successful.
- Do your best to stay as fit and *young* as possible (mentally, too).
- Continue to dress the way *he* likes (all day, all night).
- Allow him his girlie magazines (but only if he *really* needs them).
- Hang out with the friends who have older wives or girlfriends.
- Tell him only a "real man" has the strength to be loyal.

SOME THINGS TO TWEAK

Me! Me! Me! Selfishness is an acceptable quality for young tykes, but when an Aries man continues to put himself first, way beyond diapers, he misses out on a lot of rewarding opportunities and friendships. Yes, he wants to charge ahead and claim victory. But try showing him how much easier the path to success would be if he would be a tad more diplomatic and cooperative. He knows how wonderful it is to feel worthy and admired, so why doesn't he think others would like to feel the same way? If he could somehow manage to treat others like human beings instead of potential rivals, he would be much more popular and in demand. And if he could stop having to "prove" himself all the time, he wouldn't be such a sore loser. Life doesn't have to be a never-ending competition, and he doesn't need to come out first all the time. Just let him know how much more incredibly *attractive* he becomes when he is more considerate of others (including yourself), and he may finally listen!

Then it would be kind of you to try broadening your Ram's outlook on life. He often lives and operates on such a basic plane, totally indifferent to spiritual matters and some of the more complex human issues that make life so rich. Conversations with him can become annoying, if not enraging, since he sees everything in such a black-and-white context. What's worse is that he won't even hear your side, so convinced is he of his own "intellectual" superiority. It would help if you could try getting him involved in some mind-expanding activities so his conclusions are more interesting than winners/losers, young/old, superior/inferior, right/wrong, yesterday/tomorrow, etc. And let him know that he can't possibly always be right. Still, the Ram thinks he's just fine as he is and won't appreciate a kick in the butt, so be *very careful* when handling him.

AND HAPPILY EVER AFTER . . .

So, you see, the years to come will keep you busy. How lucky for you that your Aries husband will inspire you to always look and be your best. Now you have real motivation to take destiny in your hands and do what it takes to make a life together as the World's Greatest/Sexiest/Mightiest Couple (at least let him dream). Plus, you have no excuse to blow it, because you know him so well by now—he just wants to be the perfect male. And it would be nice if you could be the perfect female, too. Feed his ego, make him feel important, and make him feel sexy. You don't want to let this man slip away, because there are few as attractive as he.

Taurus, the Bull

(about April 21 till about May 21)

The Taurus man is great boyfriend material. Affectionate and stable, he has respect for money, simple pleasures, and love. And like the Bull, he's an uncomplicated creature, content to graze on his terrain—unless he's incited into one of his famous, but rare, tantrums. Otherwise he's pretty tame and seeks an affectionate woman with whom to share the joys of life. And unlike some other men out there, the Taurus man truly appreciates the benefits of a warm and secure relationship that has long-term potential.

The Bull strives for comfort, beauty, and material success, and wouldn't it be a bonus if he could find all of this in a partner—a sensual, attractive female who already has money (or knows how to make and invest it)? Okay, this might be a greedy Bull's fantasy, but a girl with at least two of these qualities stands a good chance of capturing this man's heart, so he's not that unreasonable.

This man tends to admire girls "with class." But that's *natural* girls with class, not the kind who wear three inches of makeup and miniskirts at eight in the morning, or who are all puffed up and pooped out after a heavy night of partying. No, the Taurus man likes the healthy, radiant woman, one who knows how to enjoy the good life (food, wine, chocolate, the works) without going overboard. Still, he has nothing against a little glamour, and some of the more flamboyant Bulls even fall for "star"-type females. But even these women have to have their feet on the ground if a long-term relationship is ever to work.

Some people accuse the Bull of being slow, especially when adapting to new situations. And maybe it's true. But he's not in a rush and he knows that a calm mind makes for good decisions. After dating more aggressive men, you may think this Bull is not interested in you. Not true. He simply needs time to get to know you, and to figure out if you belong to his herd. Once in love, however, he won't let go of you easily. And you don't have to worry about getting dumped after the first time in bed. This man usually thinks of the longer term, in both work and love.

Financial security is very important to him, and a poor Bull is not a happy Bull. Still, his needs are usually reasonable. Generally, as long as he can acquire the house of his dreams, have mountains of cash in the bank, and maintain a very comfortable standard of living, he stays satisfied. Still, his respect (maybe adulation!) for the greenback is unusually high, so any potential girlfriend will have to demonstrate an equal respect for it. This is not the man who will appreciate frivolous spending sprees and empty bank accounts, so be warned, you gals of the sort whose money burns through pockets!

No, this man is not stingy. He enjoys offering perfume, jewelry, and quality purses to his girlfriend, but he's not the type to spend a fortune on senseless experiences, because he wants his hard-earned money to show for something. And nothing will endear a Taurus's heart more than a woman who understands the value of money and knows how to stretch that dollar! The good thing is that you'll never have to worry about this guy struggling with debt and risky ventures—he's just too sensible to get himself into hot water. And if somehow he *does* get into trouble, he usually has the financial savvy to pull himself out. Just be aware that, to this man, everything has a monetary value, and you may well deduce your own worth (at least through his eyes) by how much he spends on you. Obviously, it would be discouraging to learn that his last date got treated to a movie premiere and dinner if you're offered only a bargain matinee and popcorn. Something to think about.

The Taurus man likes stability, routine, and simplicity (and this includes a good tumble in the hay). After dating him for a while, some girls accuse him of being too settled, even boring. True, this is not the man who will head for the disco and rage till dawn—his idea of a great evening is a cozy night at home with his girlfriend, indulging in good food, good wine, and good sex. Or a barbecue with close friends. Just don't let him lapse into grandpa mode, and forbid the worn-out slippers! Encourage him to leave the house for an antiques auction, or even a party. He enjoys social get-togethers when hosted by intimate friends with taste.

Yes, the Bull is one of the most simple creatures around. And he's generally good-humored, until the day someone encroaches upon his territory, trying to claim any of his possessions (including his girlfriend). Ever see a mad Bull? Scarier than a wounded Scorpion! Within seconds, this oasis of calm can explode into one of the most terrifying of storms. But he usually regains his tranquillity in a reasonable amount of time. And he knows how to forgive (though he never forgets).

When a Taurus man feels betrayed by a loved one, he usually succumbs to a bull-headed silence. And since he doesn't talk about it, his injured feelings can brew inside until he is sick with grief. The unhappy Bull needs loads of physical affection and loving reassurance in order to find his smile again. And when his sweetheart is down in the dumps, the Taurus man will reach out and comfort her with his rich, soothing voice. Though he appears rock solid, this creature has a tender heart.

If you want a Taurus man, be prepared to be possessed like any of his other objects. And try to forgive him (or at least tolerate) his moments of stubbornness. He might not be for every gal, but for those of you seeking a good old-fashioned guy and long-term benefits, this man is worth seducing.

THE TAURUS MAN IS

AT BEST	AT WORST
Sensual	Possessive
Affectionate	Resentful
Devoted	Materialistic
Solid	Greedy
Practical	Self-Indulgent
Reliable	Slow
Hardworking	Boring
Determined	Inert
Loyal	Stubborn
Natural	Unoriginal
Productive	Unspiritual
Realistic	Jealous
Artistic	Bullying
Musical	Lazy
Easygoing	Gluttonous

SOME FAMOUS TAURUS MEN

Tony Blair, Jay Leno, Billy Joel, Andre Agassi, Pope John Paul II, George Clooney, Pierce Brosnan, Jerry Seinfeld, Al Pacino, Jack Nicholson, Alessandro Scarlatti, Karl Marx, Adolf Hitler, William Shakespeare, Niccolò Machiavelli, Steve Winwood, Enrique Iglesias, Daniel Day-Lewis

MUST HAVE BEEN A TAURUS MAN

Gordon Gekko *(Wall Street)* (okay, a *very* greedy Taurus!)

THE SEDUCTION

The single Bull is always ready for romance, so an attractive female will never go unnoticed. In fact, this is the guy who can develop those really big crushes (like the kind you had when you were fifteen), even on a girl he barely knows. The problem is, he's not always sure of himself, so he won't necessarily show his interest until he's had enough time to figure out if he even has a chance. Still, you can't be blind to the smile that warms his face when you say hello, or the kind attention he pays when you need help, so don't mistake his lack of aggression for indifference.

If this Bull is interested, he'll quickly learn your little habits and know where he can casually "bump" into you. Most Bulls need to develop a pleasant rapport before asking a girl out on a date, so don't destabilize him with bizarre or dualistic behavior. Return his smiles, make him feel comfortable around you, and delight him with an occasional physical touch (brushing the hair out of his eyes, or adjusting his jacket) so he feels encouraged to ask you out.

When you do finally date, *show* him (don't tell him) that you enjoy his company and find him attractive. Body language counts big time with this fella, so use yours to express your interest. And make sure that first kiss is for real. This man loves luscious, sensual kisses, and lots of lip (versus tongue), so indulge in long make-out sessions, the kind that make him weak in the knees.

After a traditional courting period (probably after he's met your mother), and only when the moment is ripe, seduce each other after great food and wine in a sensual or natural environment. Take your time, draw out your most feminine side, and let him enjoy every inch of your body. And know that now that he's had you, you're *his*!

DOS AND DON'TS OF A GREAT RELATIONSHIP

DO

Be feminine and sensual.
Be loyal and devoted.
Be affectionate and loving.
Be good with money.
Know how to entice him.
Appreciate music or art.
Love food and wine.
Enjoy cozy nights before the fire.
Strive for comfort and harmony.
Have quality friends.
Know how to give a great dinner party.
Stand by your principles.
Appreciate the beauty of nature.
Treat his home with respect.
Know how to kiss (and give killer massages).

DON'T

Be flighty or frivolous.
Be cold or aloof.
Be too cerebral or abstract.
Be unstable or flaky.
Be reckless with money.
Be disloyal or dishonorable.
Be stingy with physical affection.
Be a party animal and live for the night.
Chum around with ex-boyfriends.
Associate with unsavory characters.
Spend more time with your girlfriends than with him.
Betray him in any way.
Go looking for arguments and disputes.
Whittle your time away.
Try to force him out of his natural rhythm.

SEX

slow, sensual, earthy, physical

This Bull enjoys all the simple pleasures of life, and sex is at the top of the list, along with food and wine. And, like his meals, sex does not have to be sophisticated or complex, just constant and satisfying. Whetting his appetite with some good foreplay is the best way to ensure an entirely delicious experience, so there's no reason to rush to the best part.

Still, before he can really enjoy sex with a girl, he has to feel comfortable with her. And it might take time to figure out what works in bed. But once he's found it, he'll want to indulge in long, luscious, even decadent lovemaking. He'll be delighted to discover his woman is equally indulgent. He also has something of an oral fixation, so allow him to kiss you wherever he wants. And feel free to explore his body with your lips. He's not shy of the naked body, and there's no part of it that should be off limits.

You can enjoy great sex in just about any natural spot. This is not the nighttime-only guy, who insists on a dark room or crisp bedsheets. Sex can transpire in a garden, on the beach, or in a barn, even in broad daylight. So save the artifice for another man and let this one bring out the animal in you.

BEST WAYS TO IMPRESS

Have clever investment strategies and a growing portfolio.
Own a house worthy of the *Architectural Digest* cover.
Have Venus-like voluptuous proportions.
Have a very rich father.
Make a home like Martha Stewart.

BEST WAYS TO GET DUMPED

Steal his credit cards and max them out.
Join a spiritualistic, money-sapping cult.
Become part of the frozen-TV-dinner movement.
Let him see the dilapidated dump you live in.
Show zero interest, even disdain, for food and other pleasures of the table.

FASHION

The Taurus man has a weakness for a beautifully dressed woman, probably because he's so into visuals. But he's not a big sucker for fashion—to him, quality is more important than quantity or the latest trend. And he's impressed by a woman who is savvy enough to spot a priceless piece at a bargain price. Anyway, it's not necessary to have a huge wardrobe, just a few great outfits. And because he gets attached to things he loves, you can never wear his favorite suede jacket too often.

Unsurprisingly, he favors classic yet feminine clothes, the kind that suggest some healthy curves without forcing them down his throat. And the Bull has nothing against the finest, most touchable fabrics, like cashmere, silk, mohair, suede, and top-grade cotton. In fact, anything synthetic, rough, or itchy would offend his tactile sense, so save your vinyl black skirt for another man. Whatever you wear, you want to look delicious, sensual, and feminine, never over-the-top or embarrassing.

As for accessories, less is more. A beautiful handbag, one expensive piece of jewelry, or a cashmere shawl can go a long way, so there's no reason to decorate yourself like a Christmas tree. And don't forget to appeal to his olfactory sense, too—a vanilla-based perfume would surely tickle his nose.

GIFT IDEAS: Those that pertain to the senses, or those that age (and appreciate) well with time. *Quality* is the operative word.

BEER BUDGET

Beautiful potted plant
Fine chocolate
Scented massage oil
Subscription to financial magazine
A deluxe massage
Illustrated book (antiques, country homes, famous artists, etc.)

CHAMPAGNE BUDGET

Expensive French wine
Cashmere sweater (or cashmere anything)
Crocodile wallet
Antique vase
Expensive tree (if he has a garden)
Blue-chip stock certificates

ADD SOME SPICE

When your relationship starts feeling too "settled" or "routine," you might be dying to add some spice. Just know that your Bull is happy with things the way they are and won't appreciate too much zestiness.

Some Ideas

1. Be friendly with an attractive (rich) man at a party, then let your Bull play out his possessiveness in the bedroom.
2. Take off on a vacation with "the girls," then call and tempt him to take the next plane to join you.

3. Take a week out of the workaday routine and explore new restaurants, friends, and places.
4. Turn up the heat by challenging him to buy you that beautiful watch you've been eyeing lately.

IF YOU SENSE A LOOMING BREAKUP

The Bull doesn't fall out of love overnight—it's more like erosion than a ticking time bomb. And he often stays in an unhappy relationship months after he should have broken up, not because he's too nice, but because he dislikes ruptures and changes to his routine. And it's a good thing, because it leaves you plenty of time to sense forthcoming trouble and get your act together.

Danger Signs to Watch For

- Increasing stubbornness
- A tightening wallet
- Fewer kisses (though the sex can continue)
- Growing coldness

If you don't want it to end, try to figure out what went wrong in the first place. You can even ask him, calmly, over a nice cozy dinner. The biggest obstacle would be long-term incompatibility. If he thinks there's no future because of an insurmountable obstacle (e.g., your child from another marriage, his family's dislike for you, your destructive spending habits, etc.), then wise up and let him go. But if the problem is easy to sort out and change, things could be looking good again very soon.

If you're too proud to confront him or (for whatever reason) unable to "talk about it," just change your daily pattern and destabilize him a bit. Spend less time with him and more time at work (making money—and lots of it). Invest in some beauty treatments and beautiful clothes. Go out more with your friends. Just inch away from him slowly so his whole routine is thrown into question. If after this you still haven't made an impact, start hanging around an attractive, rich-looking male. And if this can't stir him to repossess you, then blow your Bull a kiss and move on to greener pastures.

For a Bull, it's usually over when it's over, especially if he falls in love with someone else. No use waiting around, either, because his next relationship could last years. If you're really stuck on him, just pray his latest love is only a rebound and that he comes running back into your arms. Otherwise, the only hope for getting him back in the future would be to achieve something amazing, like starting a company and making it into the Fortune 400.

AND NEVER FORGET

His essential need for financial security

HOW MR. TAURUS SEES YOU

	AT BEST	AT WORST
Aries	stimulating, motivating	belligerent, hurried
Taurus	sensual, dependable	obstinate, bullying
Gemini	flirty, youthful	unreliable, whimsical
Cancer	nurturing, soft	inconstant, unrealistic
Leo	classy, warm	bossy, unyielding
Virgo	dependable, economical	prudish, carping
Libra	feminine, aesthetic	flittering, superficial
Scorpio	devoted, profound	rebellious, hurtful
Sagittarius	simple, natural	meandering, irresponsible
Capricorn	ambitious, wise	unaffectionate, harsh
Aquarius	easygoing, kind	aloof, unpossessible
Pisces	enchanting, romantic	impractical, dishonest

COUPLES COMPATIBILITY

BEST BETS	WHY NOT?	CHALLENGING
Cancer	Aries	Aquarius
Virgo	Taurus	
Leo	Pisces	
Scorpio	Sagittarius	
Capricorn	Libra	
	Gemini	

TAURUS MAN (Billy Joel) and AQUARIUS WOMAN (Christie Brinkley)

What an oddball couple—these two signs couldn't be more different! But that doesn't mean they can't be attracted to each other, even in a *big* way. The Aquarius woman is drawn to anything out of the norm—she's the type who thinks there's something really cool about rock stars (at least until the novelty wears off). And no Taurus man can resist a beautiful (and financially successful) model. The difference is that he's in a relationship for the long term, but Ms. Aquarius can't commit to "forever" (or even next year). If Mr. Taurus would try to be a bit more original, unpredictable, and less possessive, he might be able to keep her intrigued in the future. But this simple creature can't change, even if he wants to. As for him, he might sing, "I love you just the way you are," but you can bet that Ms. Aquarius's aloofness and erratic behavior really get to him after a while. Even though these signs make for an interesting couple, the long-term prospects are grim indeed! (And they're even worse when the man is the Aquarius and the woman is the Taurus.)

SOME ADVICE—TAKE IT OR LEAVE IT

YOUR SIGN	
Aries	DO: motivate him to attain his financial goals DON'T: be too impatient if things go slower than you want
Taurus	DO: share in your love of the good life DON'T: let your relationship get too boring and routine
Gemini	DO: direct your intellect toward finance and investing DON'T: drive him insane by changing your mind every five seconds
Cancer	DO: create a cozy environment with lots of goodies DON'T: destabilize him with your changing moods
Leo	DO: delight him with your passionate lovemaking DON'T: become a little dictator and give orders
Virgo	DO: enjoy a healthy and simple life together DON'T: berate him for his occasional overindulgences
Libra	DO: play up your love of beauty and harmony DON'T: fritter away his money on your luxuries
Scorpio	DO: impress him with the intensity of your love DON'T: go looking for trouble or provoke him into a rage
Sagittarius	DO: share your love of the good life and the outdoors DON'T: seek adventure now that you're in a relationship
Capricorn	DO: display your loyal, steady nature DON'T: deny him the physical affection he needs
Aquarius	DO: try to be a little more dependable DON'T: disappoint him with your need for loose strings
Pisces	DO: seduce him with your tender love DON'T: live in a fantasy world

Looking Farther Down the Road

THE ENGAGEMENT

This man needs to test out your long-term potential before making any major decisions, so don't expect a proposal overnight. Just be happy to know that you're quite safe with a Taurus man. If you've been with him for a while and you're certain your relationship is getting better each day, then sit back and relax. A satisfied Bull is not the type to suddenly drop you after two years (unless you shock him with some truly unacceptable behavior), so don't panic if things are progressing at a snail's pace.

If you've waited long enough, though, give him a little push in the butt before he gets too settled the way things are. You might want to announce a potential threat to "his property," like an out-of-state job offer or the return of a long-lost boyfriend. And if you're really confident, you can even give him an ultimatum. Just don't think you'll impress him by wild and careless actions—he needs to be convinced you have long-term value.

THE WEDDING

The Taurus man plans on marrying for life, so take all the time you'll need to plan the celebration of his life. Besides, he's in no rush—marriage means major change, so he could use plenty of time to acclimate to his upcoming status. Just don't unsettle him by changing the plans ten times a day or wasting deposits left and right. If you can prove your financial savvy now, the engagement period should stay serene and blissful.

This is the guy who appreciates the type of wedding many girls dream about—traditional, romantic, and intimate. And this is the right day to showcase your great taste. Just make sure it's all about quality rather than quantity—that means no skimping on the food, wine, or cake. A hungry Bull is never a happy Bull, and this should be one of the happiest days of his life.

THE HONEYMOON

The Bull will be happy to leave his own habitat for such an intimate trip, but try to remember to pack the one thing he's stuck to—like his favorite pillow or the robe he cannot live without. This will be a wonderful time to strengthen the bond of love, so plan a romantic trip that's not too hectic. This trip is more about love and intimacy than anything else.

Unless he has a pressing job to get back to, your Taurus husband will be happy to hang out with you for as long as his wallet permits. Even if there's not much to do. As long as he establishes his little habits and discovers how to obtain his creature comforts early on, he'll be content. He might even pack on a few pounds in a very short time. Allow him to indulge himself and don't go poking at his love handles—honeymoons only come around once in a lifetime, and he wants to make the most out of it.

Honeymoon Sex

Good, lusty sex should be the highlight of the trip. Especially in the midafternoon, following a great lunch. This could happen in any natural setting—on a secluded sandy beach, in a hot tub, or on a lovers' chaise under the shade of a tree. So don't worry about any formalities—sex should just be natural and physically satisfying. And if you're extra confident, you could lounge around all day in your birthday suit.

MAKING IT IN THE LONG HAUL

When the newlywed period is over, you can enjoy the coming years without much worry. Your Taurus husband has no problems "settling" into married life, and will be delighted if you adjust easily as well. As long as you provide him a stable, loving home life, without too many surprises and too many bills, he should continue to thrive well into middle age. And if problems do arise, they'll often be related to finances or disloyal behavior. Just make sure you keep your feet on the ground and things should go swell.

DOS AND DON'TS FOR LASTING BLISS

DO

Give him plenty of physical affection.
Respect his habits and timetables.
Be a value shopper and know how to spot a bargain.
Engage in an activity that has moneymaking potential.
Try to cultivate a green thumb in the garden.
Put time into creating the home of his dreams.
Sharpen your culinary skills and cook your way into his heart.
Provide the creature comforts he craves.
Spend time with quality, true friends.
Host great dinners in your attractive home.
Make long-term plans together.
Know how to enjoy the simple things in life.
Make up and cuddle after having a fight.
Take up an artistic hobby (if you have the talent).
Show him you love him.

Get into debt.
Whittle away your time on nonproductive activities.
Change your plans every five minutes.
Make promises you can't keep.
Make your home a mess.
Spend too many nights out with your girlfriends.
Live an unstructured, undisciplined life.
Be stingy with your love.
Ever take his opponent's side.
Press him to make hasty decisions.
Look for reasons to fight when none exist.
Get friendly with ex-boyfriends.
Seek constant thrills and adventures.
Let arguments go unresolved for too long.
Neglect your appearance for too long.

EARTHLY BLISS (AKA SEX)

Earthly is the right word for the sensual Taurus man. To him, sex is one of the most natural acts in the world, and more physical than anything else. No, when it comes to lovemaking, he doesn't need to reach spiritual dimensions. Sex just needs to *feel* good. And this man, who has a profound love of the female body and enough time to enjoy it, has the capacity to appreciate sex more than most other men (at least in the physical sense).

As time goes on, he will be even more attuned to your body, more sensitive to your erogenous zones and what turns you on. Don't be shy about what you want—go ahead and tell him to lick your toes if that really gets you going. Though the sex will not only satisfy but improve with time, you might eventually introduce a little novelty to keep it interesting—but nothing kinky, like sex toys or leather and chains. Try something that will enhance the sensual experience, be it incense, erotic music, body oil, or whipped cream. Make sex with you as indispensable as the greenback, and your Bull will never go astray.

And make sure to keep it regular. If he's used to sex three times a week, then try to maintain that quota. There's nothing erratic about his sense of timing, so it wouldn't do to have sex every day for a week, then none for a month. Even when you're going through a busy period, set aside time for sex if it's on the unwritten agenda. You wouldn't want to leave this warm-blooded animal cold.

AND CHEATING . . . ?

Having an eye (and a weakness) for natural beauty, your Bull might lust for an exceptionally attractive woman, but he's normally too sensible to risk the stability of his home and marriage for the fleshly pleasures of a one-night stand. Especially if he's of the more common breed—the one who has a good job and a reasonable appetite. Just think, one mistake could feasibly lead to a messy and expensive divorce. And even if he is protected by a prenup, there's the house to think about, the kids' welfare, and all the rest. No, you don't have to spend sleepless nights worrying about whether this Bull will stay true, because he's put too much into the relationship to botch it up now. Besides, he's not fond of change, especially when his life is fully established and he's at least reasonably happy.

But if he happens to be a Taurus of the more artistic nature, a real *bon vivant,* his senses might overrule his reason and he could easily commit a wine-induced sin with a voluptuous creature. Still, there's really no reason to fret about things beyond your control. Just keep your Taurus husband content and satisfied so he has no reason to stick his nose elsewhere. He's a simple creature, after all, and one of the most loyal, too.

REASONS HE MIGHT CHEAT

- If he's not getting enough love and attention
- If he's overcome by his senses
- If he needs to get back at you for disloyal behavior
- If you don't connect on long-term goals anymore (this could lead to cheating *and* divorce)

WHAT YOU CAN DO

- Satisfy all his sensual needs.
- Remind him how important fidelity is to you.
- Let him at least look at attractive women.
- Make your home so cozy that he has no desire to leave.
- Find the time for romance in a busy world.
- Convince him of your loyalty.
- Surprise him at the office with home-made lunches.
- Maintain your beauty regimen.
- Give him regular out-of-this-world massages.

SOME THINGS TO TWEAK

The Bull has an unhealthy tendency to measure his happiness and self-worth by the size of his house and the money in his bank account. The sooner you make him realize that it's not all about money and possessions, the sooner he'll evolve into a more interesting person. And if the Bull's quest for money and acquisitions becomes so dominating that he forgets the pleasure he once had in a simple picnic, force him out of his office and back outdoors so he can marvel at the power of nature (with which he is intimately linked). Remind him, with a great bottle of red wine and some incredibly luscious kisses, that the most rewarding things are within his immediate grasp. Give him some great books to read (but nothing about finance or investing) and listen to music he used to love. Do everything you can to free him of his captivity to greed and materialism so he can grow into a happier and more multidimensional human being. He'll adore you for making him a better person!

Then you could also try working on his resistance to change. The Bull likes his life just the way it is, not necessarily because it's the best setup, but because it's what he knows and trusts. It can get to the point, though, where structures he once had in place no longer work and are actually holding him back from true happiness. Encourage him to look at change as something that can be positive and even necessary (unless "change" means finding a new woman!). It might help to introduce a little spontaneity into his life now, so that he could be a little more ready for change later.

AND HAPPILY EVER AFTER . . .

A lifetime with a Bull won't resemble anything like your favorite soap opera, with intrigues unfolding by the hour, but at least you can gain some inner tranquillity by knowing you have an above-average chance of staying together in the long run. And eventually you'll probably own a beautiful home together (while your other married friends are still renting or filing for bankruptcy). So concentrate on your home, garden, kitchen, children, and growing bank account if that's what he wants—is it really too much to ask of you? Hopefully not. Feel lucky you have a reasonable and loyal husband who will keep the money rolling in.

Gemini, the Twins

(about May 22 till about June 21)

A Gemini man? Double fun—or double trouble! It won't take you gals long to find out that you are dealing not with one man, but two (maybe even more). Just when you think you know him, this Twin will surprise you with another face. So be prepared for a series of tricks and turns, changes and indecision. Life is never simple with a Gemini man!

You probably met this Twin through friends or work, as he is super well connected and knows a zillion people. Yes, there's something fresh and youthful about him, despite his age. This guy is lots of fun—he's great for parties and cocktails, and is usually invited everywhere. Most of all, the Gemini man is interesting, and has a great command of many different subjects (though the depth of his knowledge leaves something to be desired).

A real city boy, this guy loves to talk, visit friends, buzz around, and keep abreast of the latest developments. And you never see him without his cell phone(s) and a couple of buddies (of both sexes), because the Gemini man *hates* to be alone. So where do you fit into this picture? Well, you will have to fit in with his gang and be able to delight his entourage with smart banter and novel ideas. No boring girls, please! And no overly physical ones. The Gemini man is ruled by his head, not passion, and the way to seduce him is to stimulate his mind, even if it takes little tricks and intrigues. You'll know this man is aroused by the glint in his eye, reflecting the thoughts shooting through his brain like comets.

As this is the man of communication, don't be surprised if you "talk" more by e-mail and telephone than face-to-face. He is not someone who needs unwavering eye contact in order to bond. And a lot of your dates may involve other couples or a group of people. (The romantic dinner à deux in a secluded restaurant will occur more often in your dreams than in reality.) A Gemini man doesn't need a magical atmosphere to find romance—he can be just as delighted in a crowded bar, a busy airport lounge, or at the intersection of a bustling street. He lives in the here and now and can enjoy his girl's company in everyday situations.

There's not really a "type" of girl he likes. He loves variety and will go from one girl to the next. Blondes, redheads, brunettes, vamps, prudes, intellectuals, athletes, lawyers, writers—each girl has something new to offer the curious Twin, who delights in discovering what makes each one tick. But there has to be a good intellectual rapport. Otherwise the Twin will be bored and move on, and you wouldn't want that to happen if you like this guy.

Still, think twice before you let him intrigue you. The Gemini man is quick and intelligent and has a way with words, making him the perfect salesman (or clever con artist). He has a knack for being able to change his words and manipulate those of others in order to finally get the reaction he wants. This might be great in politics or sales, but hard on the gals who fall for him, for they never quite know where they stand with this man.

Fidelity is also an issue here, as the Gemini man is one of the quickest to cheat on his girlfriends, knowing he can extricate himself from trouble with one of his clever lies. (Be suspicious when he suddenly breaks a date for a "business dinner," or tells you the girl you saw him lunching with is just an "old friend" or his college roommate's sister!) It's not that the Gemini man is a bad person, it's simply that he doesn't really know what he wants. Maybe we should just feel sorry for him, for they say that the Gemini man is on a lifelong search for the lost twin he'll never find.

Because of his dual nature, the Gemini man is not the most dependable. He can make a date or appointment, only to cancel it at the last moment (or not even show up). Maybe he was one person when making the date, then another person when the day arrived. Or maybe something more "interesting" came up. The Twin doesn't give a second thought to changing plans, and will be surprised to learn you were upset when he did. He just doesn't take things that seriously, including the words "I love you," which he can utter while thinking of another girl. But he does take his communication skills seriously and can count on winning back your heart. Just make sure you *never* reveal your deepest secrets and fears, because he won't hesitate to share them with others when you break up. (If you really do want the whole world to know you spent a

THE GEMINI MAN IS

AT BEST	AT WORST
Intelligent	Frivolous
Curious	Superficial
Adaptable	Two-Faced
Quick-Witted	Insecure
Logical	Nosy (or Meddlesome)
Articulate	Inconsistent
Amusing	Restless
Youthful	Nervous
Inquisitive	Cunning
Lively	Dishonest
Agile	Unreliable
Clever	Gossipy
Multifaceted	Capricious
Fun	Immature

night in jail back in your wild days, just tell it to your Gemini lover, who will have the word out faster than CNN). On the flip side, he'll be sure to spread the word about some of your more shining achievements, so go ahead and brag about your new promotion if you want your rivals to hear about it.

Despite the Twin's contradictory behavior, he really would like to fall in love. And though he fears commitment, he craves it at the same time. The nearest thing to his soulmate is out there, and if he is lucky enough to find her, he will do everything to keep her. If you think that girl is you, do everything you can to keep the relationship dynamic and interesting (whatever that means to your particular Twin). Some gals love the challenge presented by the Gemini man and are eager to play constant mind games and keep him on his toes (hey, not all girls are simple!). Other girls of a more serious vein will quickly tire of the games and move on.

SOME FAMOUS GEMINI MEN

Bob Hope, Rudy Giuliani, Donald Trump, Johnny Depp, Newt Gingrich, Paul McCartney, Clint Eastwood, Liam Neeson, Michael J. Fox, Prince, Bob Dylan, Henry Kissinger, John Wayne, Ian Fleming, John F. Kennedy, Walt Whitman, George Bush, Jacques Cousteau, Mike Meyers, Errol Flynn, Rupert Everett, Trent Lott

MUST HAVE BEEN A GEMINI MAN

Jerry Maguire *(Jerry Maguire)*

THE SEDUCTION

To get the Twin's attention, you'll need to appear interesting yet mysterious, so he's dying to figure you out. Once he's decided you're worth the effort, he'll delight in planning a customized seduction. For one girl, it's the buddy approach; for another, it's the flirtatious-fool approach; for the more spoiled gals, the now-you-see-me-now-you-don't game. This guy loves discovering what makes each girl tick—it's at least half the fun of dating. He might even enlist the aid of friends (or the Internet) to dig up inside info on you that will help him plan his next moves. (One sometimes wonders if he doesn't get more satisfaction in scheming his seductions than concluding them in the bedroom.)

Instead of asking you out on a date, the Twin might try testing you out among a group of people. But the time and place are unimportant. No matter when, how, or where you finally interact, make sure you dazzle the pants off him without giving yourself away. And without giving direct answers to his (often annoying) questions. And without making him certain he has a chance. You must intrigue him, then send him home with a million questions buzzing around in his head. Ideally, he even loses a night of sleep, tossing and turning in his bed. (And maybe he has the dark circles to prove it the next morning.)

If you haven't managed to *bore* your Gemini friend already, you're in for a delightful courtship—e-mails, phone calls, parties, friends, surprises. . . . Enjoy his attention, continue to flirt, but keep it "unofficial" and fun for a while. There's no reason to lose your head now. Not now and not ever.

And yet when the time feels right to take things to the bedroom (or wherever else), throw caution to the wind and enjoy yourself. Remember, the Twin doesn't take life *that* seriously. So stop being a prude and have some fun. Just don't start thinking commitment yet. Remember, today is today and tomorrow is tomorrow.

SEX

quick, varied, versatile

Not highly sexed, the Gemini man is more comfortable in the art of flirting, which he really has down. The intellectual seduction is his forte, and his fun kisses are sure to delight. Once alone in a bedroom, though, he may disappoint. It's not that he doesn't enjoy sex, it's just that he finds it less interesting than seduction and clever repartee. Besides, the most unoriginal act in the world can become boring after a while.

This doesn't mean he's indifferent to sex. It's just not his reason for living. And he's not as interested in the physical aspect of it as some other men are. For him, sex is about discovering the woman you are, and what differentiates you from all the others. So there's a lot of cerebral activity going on up there while you're both at it. And not just pertaining to you or your performance. For all you know, he could be analyzing the way he concluded his business meeting, wondering where he'll be having dinner that night, or musing about that fantastic girl he just met on the street. He's just that way, so don't worry if he doesn't scream your name out in a moment of passion. (But think twice if he screams out someone else's name.)

As you get to know each other, sex might become less and less interesting, so make sure you keep things refreshing by adding variety and spontaneity. And continue to go out and flirt with other clever men. Just because you're an "official" couple now doesn't mean you have to stop the games.

DOS AND DON'TS OF A GREAT RELATIONSHIP

DO

Have an e-mail address and a cell phone.
Have lots of interests and hobbies.
Be ready for last-minute plans (and adaptable to changing ones).
Be intellectually stimulating.
Be up-to-date on the latest books and world events.
Flirt with his friends (but in a harmless way).

Be on great terms with his entourage.
Play mind games and keep him on his toes.
Allow him ample time for friends and visits.
Be dazzling at parties and social events.
Share his love of the latest gossip.
Stand by your personal opinions.
Change your look frequently.
Tell him you care about him when he's feeling insecure.

DON'T

Be possessive and jealous.
Be boring and slow.
Be too emotional and clingy.
Be uneducated or unread.
Be illogical and irrational.
Demand passionate displays of love.
Be too predictable.
Fight with his friends and siblings.
Cling to his side at social gatherings.
Say the wrong things at a dinner party.
Believe everything he says.
Press for commitment.
Drop your friends or hobbies for him.
Harass him for innocent flirting.
Tell him your secrets—ever!

BEST WAYS TO IMPRESS

Have a more spectacular social agenda than his.
Have a string of degrees by age twenty-six.
Be able to charm your way into *any* place, location, or event.
Be a world-renowned, well-connected journalist.
Win a Pulitzer Prize.

BEST WAYS TO GET DUMPED

Just sit there and look pretty.
Live in a fantasy world.
Become a mute.
Be voted "Biggest Dud."
Be computer illiterate.

FASHION

The Twin is not obsessed with fashion, but because he tends to be up-to-date on just about everything, he might know if you're sporting last year's look. That's why the best bet is clothes with a modern edge or even a trendy twist. Quantity and versatility take priority over quality, so ditch the designer vintage coat you wear every day and expand your options.

Dressing up can become fun again and you can experiment with different looks—one day the brainy CEO and the next day the urban vamp. What it really comes down to is changing your look often so you continue to keep him intrigued. Just never strive to look old and frumpy.

As for accessories, the Twin prefers the minimalist look, and anything in silver or platinum tones. That means saying "no" to the gaudy red baubles you picked up at the flea market, or Granny's favorite brooch. Sure, a trendy bag or necklace might delight, but keep it simple and young. And you certainly can't go wrong with a stylish watch and cell phone, either. In case you don't have the patience to mix and match, just make sure you have a great French manicure (but keep your nails on the shorter side)—many Twins have a hand fetish.

GIFT IDEAS: Those that can aid in his quest to communicate, learn, travel, or socialize

BEER BUDGET

Latest music CD
Books (especially reference and nonfiction)
Computer software
Social organizer/address book
Walkman
Manicure set

CHAMPAGNE BUDGET

Designer pen set
Latest cell phone
High-tech daily organizer
Great watch
Overnight bag
Airfare to NY or SF

ADD SOME SPICE

This restless man has a low boredom threshold, so it's imperative to throw in some spice on a regular basis.

Some Ideas

1. Save that sparkle in your eye for another interesting man to test out your Twin's jealousy level.
2. Just when he thinks he knows you inside and out, let him catch you in a big (but not ugly) lie so he's forced to reevaluate his assessment of you. (And there's no reason to be too apologetic—he never is.)
3. Become chummy with his groupies and arrange fun activities with them when your Twin is out of town.

4. Become close, very close, to one of his ex-girlfriends, then invite her to tag along with you and your Twin—the dynamics of this bizarre triangle will set his mind buzzing!

IF YOU SENSE A LOOMING BREAKUP

It's never easy to understand the Gemini man's true intentions, even when he's planning to break up with you. He's just such a good talker and knows the right things to tell you, even when he doesn't mean them anymore, so never be smug when dating this man, no matter what he tells you. Still, a perceptive woman can tell when the Twin begins to tire of her.

Danger Signs to Watch For

- Increasing interest in others
- More jumpy eye contact and fidgeting
- More nights out with the buddies
- Increasing careless and thoughtless lies
- More nervousness and restlessness
- More last-minute changes of plans (that exclude you)

If you think your relationship is heading off the map, relieve the poor guy of his boredom and misery and disappear immediately! You can't imagine how fascinated he'll be by your rash, unexpected behavior, causing a sudden upheaval in his previous assumptions and logical conclusions. Sure, he might explain to his friends that he was going to break up with you anyway, but you can be certain he'll lose his concentration in the weeks to come as he strives to understand what happened and how he managed to misjudge you.

If curiosity gets the better of him and he demands an explanation, just tell him his once-charming immaturity began to annoy you. Or, if you really want to hurt him, tell him he's become a big *bore* (yawn). Then do a disappearing act and change your cell phone number and e-mail address. Allow him time to wallow in his innate insecurities while you charge ahead with your own agenda. And if you do want him back, reemerge onto the scene with a make-over (new hair, makeup, clothes, and attitude), hang out with different people, talk about new things, and make it very difficult for him to seduce his way back to you. By the way, this is the type of guy who *always* wants you more when he no longer has you, so be prepared for him to do or say anything to win you back.

AND NEVER FORGET

His essential need to change

HOW MR. GEMINI SEES YOU

	AT BEST	AT WORST
Aries	spontaneous, active	direct, demanding
Taurus	charming, serene	possessive, bullheaded
Gemini	lively, clever	insecure, nervous
Cancer	intuitive, capricious	clingy, overly emotional
Leo	bright, confident	overbearing, exclusive
Virgo	logical, intelligent	disciplined, dull
Libra	social, flittering	dependent, vain
Scorpio	intriguing, complex	consuming, jealous
Sagittarius	optimistic, daring	far-seeking, philosophical
Capricorn	grounding, realistic	serious, solitary
Aquarius	interesting, novel	unsettling, stubborn
Pisces	enigmatic, adaptable	irrational, melancholic

COUPLES COMPATIBILITY

BEST BETS	WHY NOT?	CHALLENGING
Aquarius	Gemini	Capricorn
Leo	Virgo	Scorpio
Libra	Cancer	Pisces
Sagittarius		Taurus
Aries		

GEMINI MAN (John F. Kennedy) and LEO WOMAN (Jacqueline Kennedy)

This couple shines brightly, at least in the public eye. The Gemini man is a great talker and can charm his way into anyone's heart. And the Leo woman, who is attracted to powerful men, has the poise and dignity to impress a nation. Together, they can make a popular pair who elicit only superlatives, which is a good thing, since both signs need to feel admired and loved. But if these people-loving people spend too much time going out and socializing, their personal lives could suffer. It doesn't help much that Mr. Gemini flirts with other women—the Leo woman expects the royal treatment from her man and becomes fierce (or ice cold) if he dares even show the slightest interest in another woman. Still, Ms. Leo has class, and will always be the "bigger" person in the end. If Mr. Gemini could save the compliments and kisses exclusively for her, Ms. Leo could give him the boost of confidence he needs and help make him a great man. Anyway, he's the lucky one in the relationship—hopefully he realizes the exceptional woman she is so he doesn't go screwing things up.

SOME ADVICE—TAKE IT OR LEAVE IT

YOUR SIGN	
Aries	DO: try to be less straightforward and more intriguing DON'T: create hostilities in his circle of friends
Taurus	DO: try adding some spontaneity and fun to your life DON'T: stick to his side at parties and make a scene if he flirts
Gemini	DO: enjoy the games but know when to draw the line DON'T: debate incessantly and end up arguing
Cancer	DO: add your intuition to his intellectual faculties DON'T: expect him to fully empathize with your feelings
Leo	DO: let him notice (and copy) your strength and loyalty DON'T: always dominate the conversation and be "right"
Virgo	DO: enjoy a mutual passion for reading and discussion DON'T: burden him with duties and deadlines
Libra	DO: have a ball together DON'T: depend on him to make you complete
Scorpio	DO: try to appreciate the lighter side of life DON'T: always suspect bad intentions and motives
Sagittarius	DO: play up your fun, adventurous side DON'T: make him feel trivial with your lofty pursuits
Capricorn	DO: impart your wisdom without seeming condescending DON'T: weigh him down with your heaviness
Aquarius	DO: know how to be his buddy DON'T: destabilize the already unstable Twin
Pisces	DO: listen and help him figure out life's dilemmas DON'T: lose yourself in an imaginary world

Looking Farther Down the Road

TRUE LOVE

THE ENGAGEMENT

As long as you continue to dazzle your Twin and make him want more, there's always the chance a proposal will come. But if your relationship begins to drag and become boring, he might just be hanging out with you until somebody more interesting comes along. If you're thinking wedding bells, don't allow a close relationship to continue for years without any commitment. This quick-witted man tends to make quick decisions, and if he really thinks you're "the one," he could pop the question in a matter of months. (Of course, he could change his mind just as fast.) But the more likely scenario is that he hesitates . . . for months, then years; and in the meantime breaks up, calls again, puts you "on hold," etc.

Sometimes the best option is to allow dating on both sides, just to test out the strength of your relationship. If he goes out with a string of duds, he may yearn for your scintillating company. And if he discovers that you've met someone more interesting (even if this someone is a figment of your imagination), he may do all in his power to flirt his way back into your heart. But if he doesn't cough up a ring after another long period, cut your losses and move on. Yeah, he can talk about marriage, muse about it, analyze it, and laud it, but talk is cheap, especially with this man. Once he stops *talking* and actually starts *doing,* you can begin to take him more seriously.

THE WEDDING

Now that you're engaged, it's time to start making wedding plans, and *fast,* before he has the chance to change his mind. You can probably consult him from time to time, but it's best to be subtle about it, otherwise you'll be constantly reminding him that a fun and diverse chapter in his life is drawing to a close. Also, don't go prancing around in joy as the wedding date approaches—he'll wonder what you're so excited about, as if you didn't have more interesting reasons to exist. In fact, it would be a good idea to immerse yourself in other activities and friendships during this time, and downplay the wedding preparations, just to keep him wondering.

This day should be happy and lots of fun, so avoid a super-formal party. As long as his zillions of friends are there to play with after the wedding vows are exchanged, your Gemini groom should be happy. If an enormous wedding tab is a problem, scrimp a bit on the food and wine. Your new husband will be so eager to mingle with friends or hit the dance floor that he'll be relieved when dinner is over.

THE HONEYMOON

The Twin is a traveling pro, so planning a great trip should be no difficult task. If you want a long honeymoon, consider multiple destinations so your Twin doesn't get restless. No matter where you decide to go, make sure there are lots of neat things to do and see. It would be brilliant of you to research your honeymoon spot well before your trip so you know just the places to go and things to do. And don't forget to introduce some fun into the agenda, like nights out at "in" restaurants and clubs.

This trip will be more about companionship and fun than love and marriage, so don't have grandiose expectations of some kind of cinematic fairy tale. Remember, you're buddies (and now buddies for life, hopefully), so strive to enjoy each other in any ordinary situation. Just see to it that he's never *bored,* or your honeymoon will be a flop. (And don't hassle him if he spends half the trip on the phone.)

Honeymoon Sex

Since sex won't be the make-it-or-break-it success factor, don't worry too much about making it perfect. If anything, strive for novelty and fun. And keep flirting with him—on the bus, at the restaurant, in the cab. Play footsies under the table, throw some looks at other men, keep him smiling. Take off for a few hours on your own, call him on his cell phone and "make love," leave him some time to read his e-mails. Just don't insist on sex every night, otherwise it becomes too routine.

MAKING IT IN THE LONG HAUL

The Twin is not very future-oriented, especially when we're talking twenty years from now, so he might not live today like someone who lives for tomorrow (and the tomorrow after that). Needless to say, you'll have the tedious job of ensuring that your relationship stays fresh and interesting once the novelty of marriage wears off. Unless you're unusually gifted, finding ways to entice your Gemini husband after ten years of marriage will be about as easy as creating fire from two rocks. Still, it's possible, but you'll definitely have to work at it.

DOS AND DON'TS FOR LASTING BLISS

DO

Challenge him with lively debates.
Stay young in spirit.
Continue to experiment with different looks.
Keep on reading and learning.
Know how to make new and interesting friends.
Plan lots of activities with fun people.
Go out at least several times a week.
Plan lots of one- or two-night getaways.
Start some new hobbies.
Flirt with other men.
Attend lots of parties and social gatherings.
Redecorate your home from time to time.
Help him make contacts for work.
Be adaptable to changing residences, if necessary.
Help him structure his time better.
Make him depend on you somehow.

DON'T

Become a complete homebody.
Explode when he flirts with other women.
Let your mutual feelings stay on the superficial level.
Get yourself in a rut (and refuse to get out).
Be less interesting than his friends' wives.
Have an emotional breakdown when it's that time of the month.
Develop a serious outlook on life.
Refuse to entertain his friends.
Snoop around his personal space and invade his privacy.
Play games if they're interfering with progress in your relationship.
Become unpopular in his circle of friends.

Take too much of his bullshit.
Make him feel that Marriage = Boredom.
Let him take too many trips without you.
Start looking or acting "old."

EARTHLY BLISS (AKA SEX)

As if you were wondering, the key to a lasting sex life is variety and surprise. The minute sex becomes routine is the minute your sex life is doomed. And it doesn't have to take all night. It can be a quickie before dinner, a handjob in the car, or an early-morning perk before work. Any uncommon experience should do the trick, so keep your options open, all the time.

There may be times when he has no interest in sex, like when he's absorbed in an engrossing novel or following the latest developments of a buddy's divorce. Fine, let him be that way. And take the opportunity to run out for a bite to eat with your girlfriends. Your sex life in the long run will never be constant. There will be periods when he wants it a lot, and periods when it's the farthest thing from his mind. But it's okay. He's a little capricious. Just accept it and don't pout when the time's not right. He'll be back on top (or side or bottom) in a matter of no time, maybe even with a new and improved technique.

Just don't make the mistake of thinking you can enslave him with your sexuality—you're dealing with a cerebral man, not a carnal animal. The only way you can have long-term power over the Twin is via the mental channel. A fantastic sex life will oblige you to use your brain as much as your body. Stimulating, teasing, playing with his mind before, during, or after sex, is the only hope for a bedazzling sex life.

AND CHEATING . . . ?

Oh, a very sensitive topic. If you want to know the absolute truth, the Gemini man is one of the more likely men to fool around. Not because he doesn't love you, but because he's more than one person. And because it's fun. But he's not the type to aggressively seek out a new girlfriend, so his intentions are not all that bad. What usually happens is that he meets other interesting gals by "accident"—at a party, a football game, the office, a restaurant. And because he's so friendly and open, these girls often pass him their cell phone numbers and e-mail addresses. It starts out very harmless, as a casual flirt. And then the e-mail exchanges begin, and the little lunch invitations, and the cell phone conversations. Soon he finds himself "involved" with another girl. But it often stays at the flirt level, with some secret kisses here and there.

Then there's the type of Gemini man who has a double life. (But chances are that your Twin does not fall into this category.) This is the Gemini man who has another relationship, or maybe more, in a different city (or state), especially one he travels to frequently for work. In case you suspect such devious behavior from your Gemini husband, be relieved to know you'll find out sooner than later. This distracted man can forget his own lies or leave evidence lying around. So eventually he'll be caught, and even his clever talk won't be able to save him.

A Gemini man will always keep you on your toes. And if you're paranoid, you might think about installing some "spy" software on his computer (though he's probably already thought about that possibility). Just keep your eyes open, check up on him from time to time, and don't fall for his clever little lies when your intuition is telling you otherwise. If you know he's fooling around, destabilize him by telling him he's free to take a hike. Sometimes it takes some drastic action to get him straight again.

REASONS HE MIGHT CHEAT

- If you become boring
- If he wants to have fun
- If his mischievous twin gets the better of him
- If he meets a girl who is drastically more interesting than you

WHAT YOU CAN DO

- Tell him you'd find out if he had another relationship.
- Keep up a lively and flirty relationship with him.
- Become very chummy with his friends (to get some inside info).
- Send him lots of witty and flirty e-mails.
- Let him see how much other men enjoy your company.
- Offer to join him on his business trips from time to time.
- Challenge him if you think he's fooling around.

SOME THINGS TO TWEAK

This guy enjoys living for the moment and playing it by ear, probably because it makes him feel carefree and young. Ask a Twin his agenda for a week from now and he's clueless (or he has an idea that will change at the last moment). Sure, there's a period in life when living day by day and making last-minute plans is okay (like in adolescence), but after that, it's time to mature, take on some responsibilities, and think longer term. In other words, *it's okay to grow up.* He won't want to hear it, so express it indirectly. Refer to the friends who are really nowhere at age forty, point out the barfly who drinks alone because he never created long-lasting and profound relationships with anyone. Just scare him into believing that the most boring and lost people out there are the ones who never took the time to build something solid (a career, house, relationship, etc.) since they were too busy changing their plans all the time. And this should make an impact, because he would rather die than be deemed *uninteresting*.

The Twin could also gain a lot by learning to trust himself instead of relying on the opinion or advice of everyone else. Should I do it? Should I take that job offer? Should I ask that girl out? Maybe not. I don't know. What do you think? I'll think about it tomorrow (and then change my mind). Listening to a Twin trying to make a decision can be exhausting. And wasteful—as if time weren't precious. Then one wonders if he even wants help, or simply wants to *talk*. But it doesn't stop there. He depends on others for amusement, for mental stimulation, for help, for filling up empty pockets of free time . . . for everything. A *big* handicap, but a temporary one if you can help him. Make a game by challenging him to do everything on his own, without the help of any friends, for an entire day. Then week. Then month. Once he realizes he can function solo, he'll actually calm down (and get more done, too).

AND HAPPILY EVER AFTER . . .

Spending your life with a Gemini man should never be dull. And you won't have to regret being bound to one man forever because you'll be married to two (at least). How many women out there can brag that they have two lovers at once? Not many, so consider yourself lucky. Just make sure you stay interesting and attractive so he considers *himself* lucky. And know how to add *some* structure to his life, but without being a party pooper. True, you may never be sure of what the future holds with this boy, but that might just keep you on your toes and young at heart. And what's wrong with that? Maybe there is some wisdom in enjoying each day as it comes, after all.

Cancer, the Crab

(about June 22 till about July 22)

Looking for someone to mother? Here's your man (boy). It's no secret that the man born under the sign of the Crab is subconsciously attached to his mother (or to his "idea" of Mother) and is often attracted to girls who remind him of her, either in character, principles, or physical resemblance. But don't cringe! He won't be secretly thinking of Mom when he romances you. He'll just bond better if he senses something in you that reminds him of his roots. You'll still be a woman to him, but one who is respected for qualities other than raw sex appeal. (Another scenario, though less frequent, is the Cancer man who wants to play Big Daddy to the helpless little girl.)

How else does this mother thing play out here? Just like Mom, the Cancer male is attracted to home, family, and childhood souvenirs. He also tends to be very protective of his loved ones and possessions. Though not an aggressive person, the Crab will come out of his shell to tenaciously defend himself and his possessions from threats, no matter how daunting, just as a mother would defend her children. Likewise, a tendency to accumulate (even hoard) money and possessions is often a priority with the Crab, so any interested girls would be wise to support this philosophy.

And like Mom, the Cancer man is sentimental. Most girls complain that their boyfriends are hopelessly forgetful of special anniversaries and occasions. Not a likely scenario with a Cancer man! He is truly romantic and nostalgic, and might send you the same bouquet of flowers on your birthday for the years to come. And he has a great memory, so don't be surprised if he remembers what you wore and the scent you carried the first time he saw you. Needless to say, first impressions are very important to this man, so never make a careless one!

The Crab often relies on his strong intuition to make decisions, which makes him shrewd in both business and love. You might be put off guard with the gentle Crab, taking him for an easy catch or rival, but you'd be very wrong to do this! While you are so busy talking in a loud voice and making big gestures, this Crab is carefully observing you, taking in each and every impression and assimilating them through his sixth sense. He never forgets the "feeling" he has, which comes in handy later on when he needs to make a move. And don't think you can fool a Cancer man with a charade, because he'll figure you out in no time. Your body language, the nuances in your voice, every

THE CANCER MAN IS

AT BEST	AT WORST
Imaginative	Moody
Intuitive	Egocentric
Emotional	Negative
Sensitive	Secretive
Protective	Touchy
Nurturing	Capricious
Enterprising	Insecure
Tenacious	Timid
Shrewd	Brooding
Cautious	Messy
Domestic	Irrational
Artistic	Childish
Sentimental	Needy
Nostalgic	Hoarding
Popular	Drifting

perceptible move you make will shed light onto your motives and feelings.

No, phony girls won't make it with this man. The females he admires are sincere, mature, and womanly. Because of the subconscious mother complex, he often dates stronger, older, richer, or taller women. And he loves nice bosoms! His woman should be stable, secure, and emotionally touchable. And an A-plus if she can cook well, too! The woman of his dreams will even go out of her way to accommodate him like Mother did (e.g., seeing to it that his clothes are always clean, that his favorite snacks are in the refrigerator, etc.). And, of course, it will be crucial that his own mom respects her.

After dating the Crab awhile, you might notice he can be a bit lunatic. No, this doesn't mean crazy, this means moody and sensitive to the phases of the moon. If you find him a little crabby at times, realize that it's probably just one of his natural mood swings. Try observing your Cancer man during the new moon and the full moon to see if you can discern a difference in his mood. And take advantage of the moments when he's at his best. They might not be around for long!

But it's true that the Crab can be overly sensitive and can lapse into one of his negative moods if you criticize him or hurt his feelings. Be careful of what you say, and reassure him if he takes something the wrong way. And if he faces public criticism (many Crabs have jobs in the public sector), be extra loving and supportive. Most of all, give him private time when he needs it—most Crabs need time for introspection and daydreaming after a busy day out in the world.

A relationship with the Cancer male can be rich and rewarding if you are the right type of girl. Family, home, material security, the past—these are the issues this man holds most at heart, and they make him a great candidate for the long term. Just hang in during his moody phases and support him during his dark moon periods. Eventually he comes out of them, and you can be sure he will never forget your emotional support.

SOME FAMOUS CANCER MEN

George W. Bush, Tom Hanks, Tom Cruise, Harrison Ford, Prince William of Wales, Ross Perot, George Michael, Chris Isaak, John Cusack, Bill Cosby, Gustav Mahler, Marc Chagall, John D. Rockefeller, Steve Forbes, the Dalai Lama, Rembrandt, Julius Caesar, Sylvester Stallone, Carlos Santana, Giorgio Armani, Duke of Windsor, Kevin Bacon, Robin Williams

MUST HAVE BEEN A CANCER MAN

Ashley Wilkes *(Gone With the Wind)*

THE SEDUCTION

The Cancer man won't notice you as much as "feel" you. If his vibes are telling him you're a *real* woman, he'll dwell on that first impression for days to come until he decides whether he should make a move. And if he does decide to make a move, he'll proceed with caution before playing out one of the many scenarios in his head. Still, his actions aren't usually direct, so his intentions might seem a little vague at first. If he seems to be spending a lot of time in your vicinity, and if he seems to enjoy your company, you can guess he's taken a liking to you.

This is one of the more traditional guys out there, so you can expect a traditional courting period. And the first dates are crucial. If you make a poor impression during any of them, he might not forgive you and decide to retreat. On the other hand, if things go well, you can expect flowers, dinners, movies, and moon-gazing. And if he suggests introducing you to his mother, you know he's getting serious. Just be sure you make a favorable impression on Mom or any other members of his family. If in doubt, play the part of the respectable lady with high standards. And don't hide that starry look in your eyes from Mom—she'll want to be assured that you have deep feelings for her son.

As soon as your Cancer boyfriend feels comfortable with you, and *only* when the time is right, let him seduce you with his tender kisses under the light of the moon, maybe after a gourmet meal (you've cooked) and a little wine. You can't imagine how important that first kiss is—he'll need to "feel" a connection with you, not only on the lip level but the emotional one, too. Soft words, cuddling, and some TLC can also play into the seduction, but they have to feel right.

Once you've established a real relationship, you can venture off to uncharted waters. But not too fast! Otherwise he'll think you're the type of "bad girl" Mom always warned him about! Use your intuition to pick up the cues and know when the moment is right. Your Cancer friend will admire your principles and know he can respect you.

SEX

emotional, tender, nocturnal

The Crab takes sex seriously, and expects a woman to have equally high standards. Any woman who jumps into bed the first night or has a casual attitude toward sex will be dismissed as "unworthy." For him, sex is more an emotional act than a physical one. And how can two people achieve emotional intimacy when they don't even know each other?

Once a Cancer man feels secure with a woman, he can express it in beautiful lovemaking, preferably at night when he's at his best. Quickies before work or in a public place are not his style. This Crab needs privacy and a safe, secret place to be able to fully indulge.

To get the most out of a sexual encounter, the mood and ambience should be romantic. Soft music, candles, some red wine, and lots of sweet nothings can lead to a fantastic and rewarding experience. Post-sex cuddling and pampering can only prolong it. Just don't expect him to talk about his feelings—you should know how to understand him without words.

DOS AND DON'TS OF A GREAT RELATIONSHIP

DO

Be sincere and true.
Be strong but caring.
Be physically and emotionally affectionate.
Enjoy home and cooking.
Support him and bolster his confidence.
Be a pillar of strength in times of crisis.
Mother him when he needs it.
Ride through his lunatic phases.
Make him feel secure and appreciated.
Allow him his private space.
Be kind to his mother and family.
Be respectful of traditions.
Be artistic or appreciative of the arts.
Learn something about history.
Encourage him to talk about his feelings sometimes.

DON'T

Criticize or nag him.
Demand logic at all times.
Be too active and independent.
Be heartless and cold.
Bring strangers into his home.
Pry at his secrets.
Demand perfect order.
Mock his emotions.
Call him a child.
Hamper his imagination.

See everything in black and white.
Use harsh, cutting words.
Neglect him when he needs attention.
Cause conflict in his inner circle.
Rock the boat unnecessarily.

BEST WAYS TO IMPRESS

Know how to cook a few Cordon Bleu recipes to perfection.
Have an impressive collection of antiques (furniture, cars, postcards, or anything else).
Write poetry, short stories, or novels (and get them published).
Live in a dream home.
Have a unique and unprecedented relationship with his mother or sister.

BEST WAYS TO GET DUMPED

Throw his family photo albums into the fire.
Tell his mother to go jump off a bridge.
Become a porn star.
Become a radical protester who gets dragged off to jail.
Pierce your tongue and nipples.

FASHION

The Crab doesn't care about the latest and most outrageous fashion trends. This is a man who admires tasteful, feminine, and ladylike clothes, à la Audrey Hepburn. He does have an artistic side, too, so nice clothes with a romantic twist are sure to delight. And beautiful vintage is always appreciated.

Still, his mother has such a (subconscious) influence over

him that he's often attracted to girls who dress in the same style she does, so if she happens to be the glamorous type, you might want to head in that direction. Even though he won't admit it, there's no doubt that Mother's wardrobe (even perfume) holds a special place in his heart.

Accessories can be artistic or antiquelike, so there's no place like a quality flea market for picking up a purse or necklace. And he just loves pieces with a "story," so go ahead and throw on the pearls you inherited from Granny. Just never go overboard with all the extras—it only gets messy and confusing. If you're not fond of accessorizing, then wear the only thing that really matters—your favorite perfume, the one you wore the first time you met and continue to wear every day.

GIFT IDEAS: Those that are intimate, historical, domestic, or sentimental

BEER BUDGET

Diary
Photo collage
Cooking spices
Swim trunks and beach gear
Books (history, autobiography, memoirs, politics, travel)
Hand-knit sweater

CHAMPAGNE BUDGET

Fine red wine
Kitchen appliances
Cashmere throw blanket
Precious bed linens
A romantic vacation
Antique furniture

ADD SOME SPICE

The Crab will add enough spice to the relationship with his changing moods, so don't stir an already rough sea. Besides, he expects you to remain stable yourself, so don't go looking for trouble. But if you can't resist . . .

Some Ideas

1. Bring out a fresh dynamic in the relationship by changing roles and playing the helpless little girl.
2. Get him to reveal one of his more naughty fantasies to you (then consider playing it out).
3. For once, don't be there for him (and let him imagine where you could be).
4. Take a trip to an unusual destination far from home and inspire him with very romantic behavior.

IF YOU SENSE A LOOMING BREAKUP

If your Crab is having serious doubts about your relationship, it won't be easy to know, because he's moody in general. And he doesn't like to talk about problems—sometimes he prefers retreating back into his safe shell. It doesn't help that he changes his mind easily, either.

Danger Signs to Watch For

- Increasing moodiness
- Increasing secrecy
- Increasingly bizarre behavior
- More unexplained absences

If you suspect your Cancer man would like to make a break, keep up a strong and loving facade. Remember, you're the stable one in the relationship, so let him see that you really are rock solid. In the end, the goal is to make him *regret* his mistake later as he looks back on your relationship with nostalgia.

The best thing to do would be to send him off into the big, wide world with your blessings. But not so carelessly! Make him a "good-bye" dinner he'll never forget—whip up his favorite dishes, play your cherished songs, give him a farewell gift and wise, loving advice for his future happiness. Just don't start to cry! Yes, he'll want to know you still love him and that you'll suffer his absence, but he can't think you're weak.

After weeks, or even months, of dating insensitive creatures, he might regret his loss and come running back to your bosom. This man is like a child who doesn't always know what he wants—sometimes he has to lose a woman before he can truly appreciate her. If he comes back, take him. Just let him know he has to start taking his responsibilities seriously and that your rules will be a little more strict in the future.

AND NEVER FORGET

His essential need for emotional and physical security

HOW MR. CANCER SEES YOU

	AT BEST	AT WORST
Aries	strong, energizing	belligerent, hasty
Taurus	conservative, loyal	bullying, inflexible
Gemini	adaptable, uplifting	cerebral, unreliable
Cancer	emotional, romantic	immature, fickle
Leo	strong, creative	egocentric, showy
Virgo	dependable, able	unfeeling, critical
Libra	romantic, diplomatic	shallow, phony

Scorpio	emotional, powerful	destructive, hurtful
Sagittarius	good-natured, happy	far-seeking, independent
Capricorn	sturdy, traditional	hard, cold
Aquarius	friendly, harmless	aloof, progressive
Pisces	fascinating, compassionate	dishonest, weak-willed

COUPLES COMPATIBILITY

BEST BETS	**WHY NOT?**	**CHALLENGING**
Scorpio	Virgo	Aquarius
Leo	Capricorn	Aries
Taurus	Cancer	Sagittarius
Pisces		Gemini
		Libra

CANCER MAN (Tom Hanks) AND SCORPIO WOMAN (Rita Wilson)

What a luscious pair! You can't imagine how perfect the Scorpio woman is for the Cancer man. When she expresses herself positively, she can be the most amazing woman, with all the qualities Mr. Cancer admires in a person: strength, conviction, devotion, passion, courage. Just as important, this is one woman who can actually *understand* the Cancer man, with all his contradictions and changing moods. A Scorpio woman doesn't even need to talk to him—she just *knows* what he's feeling. And when she loves, she loves intensely. Very comforting news for the Cancer man, who's always in need of emotional security. And a Cancer man who feels loved and appreciated can be one of the most tender and loving husbands around, with the emotional depth necessary to enchant any Scorpio woman. This is the ideal match for Mr. Cancer, the woman who can make a big man out of him. Advice for him: Don't let this one get away!

SOME ADVICE—TAKE IT OR LEAVE IT

YOUR SIGN	
Aries	DO: express your energy in a positive, inspiring way DON'T: come on *too* strong
Taurus	DO: delight him with your loving support and affection DON'T: be so pragmatic when he needs to dream
Gemini	DO: try to stop thinking and learn to start *feeling* DON'T: make him even more insecure with your flakiness
Cancer	DO: be the strong one in the couple DON'T: be helpless when he needs your help
Leo	DO: endear him with your warm support and loyalty DON'T: put your needs before his
Virgo	DO: let him know he can count on you DON'T: make him even more unsure with your cutting remarks
Libra	DO: use your innate ability to say the right things DON'T: put your social life above your relationship
Scorpio	DO: seduce him with your strength and conviction DON'T: shock him with your capacity to hurt
Sagittarius	DO: infuse him with some of your natural optimism DON'T: engage in adventurous and risky behavior
Capricorn	DO: be the pillar of strength he can always lean on DON'T: hide in your steel armor and deny him your emotions
Aquarius	DO: get in touch with your own emotions so you can sympathize with his DON'T: destabilize him with your unpredictable and independent behavior
Pisces	DO: be the woman he can bear his deepest secrets and fears to DON'T: be weak or look for the easy way out

Looking Farther Down the Road

THE ENGAGEMENT

The Cancer man takes engagements seriously, so he usually won't rush into anything until he's sure you're the one. But if his intuition assures him that you're the woman for him, even at first sight, he could propose unexpectedly—you just never know with him. Still, even in his most capricious moments, he'll subconsciously hear Mother's words of wisdom ("Never make hasty decisions, Johnny"). Whether he heeds them or not depends on his "mood."

If you've been together a long time and he's shying away from the next step, you may want to bring up the matter yourself. Just make sure you appeal to his emotions instead of to logic or reason. (Whipping out a computer list of pros and cons is not the way to go.) Gently broach the subject during an excellent home-made meal. Let him "feel" the sincerity and goodness in your heart. And always wait for the right moment.

THE WEDDING

The Cancer man will be grateful if you take care of all the arrangements. But you'd better comply if he insists on marrying in the same place his parents or grandparents did, even if it's an old barnyard. The Crab considers tradition more important than personal preferences, so you should probably consult with his mother or sisters on wedding details. Anyway, it's a family affair, and there's no reason his beloved family should be kept out of the planning.

Most likely, your Cancer man would appreciate an intimate celebration with trusted family and friends—nothing too big and noisy. What's really important is the general *mood.* Yes, your Cancer man appreciates good food and fine wine, but the overall ambience is even more important. Strive for romance and nostalgia and create an *atmosphere,* one he can savor for the rest of his life. And make sure an excellent photographer captures the mood in pictures, especially black and white. You might even want to have your wedding recorded on video.

THE HONEYMOON

This trip *must* be wonderful because special occasions are so important to the Cancer man. See to it that the romantic mood you established at your wedding carries over into your honeymoon trip, and stay attuned to your Cancer hubby's moods. Most of all, endear yourself to him with your thoughtful and responsible planning, and make sure you pack all the things he might need.

Secretly intrigued by other cultures and far-off lands, the Crab needs a few days to integrate and absorb the stimuli and impressions he receives (which he might want to get down on paper), so don't be alarmed if your new Cancer husband is particularly quiet—he's not regretting his marriage but trying to get a "feel" for this unknown habitat. And don't forget the *major* step he's just taken—the umbilical cord is cut, he's far from home and beginning to realize that his life will never be the same. Give him time to acclimate, reassure him with your loving vibes, get your trip down in photos, and give him no reason to look back.

Honeymoon Sex

This is not the moment to shock your Cancer husband with grandiose sex play or eccentric demands. Any deviant behavior could send him packing and on the next plane out! The first post-wedding sexual experience should reassure him that he's with the woman he just married, the woman he can depend on for stability and wisdom. Of course, the mood factor will play a big role in the seduction. It just has to be the right moment for magic. Dim the lights, put on "your song," showcase your comforting breasts in a flattering nightgown. Cuddle, whisper sweet somethings, exchange sips of a glass of champagne. And only when the moment is fully ripe is it time for tender and loving sex.

MAKING IT IN THE LONG HAUL

A content Crab should have no problem planting long-term roots. But he needs to feel good in his home, so don't be hasty when choosing a nest, and do your best to make it as cozy and intimate as possible. Yes, there will be bad days, even dark ones, that can drive the strongest woman insane. Just keep your cool and give him extra attention so he can find his smile again.

DOS AND DON'TS FOR LASTING BLISS

DO

Stay on excellent terms with his mother and sisters.
Cook your way into his heart.
Make plans to travel together.
Run your household like a tight ship.

Help him organize his office (and life).
Entertain at home.
Sympathize with his feelings and moods.
Endear yourself to him with thoughtful gestures.
Help him gain the confidence he needs to attain his goals.
Let him dream.
Allow him his private time when he needs it.
Reassure him if he takes something the wrong way.
Let him be immature from time to time.
Pamper and indulge him.
Save and accumulate money together.
Accept him the way he is.

DON'T

Berate him for capricious behavior (unless it's completely unreasonable).
Let him pull you down into his dark moods.
Neglect him or his needs.
Unsettle him by having a nervous breakdown.
Go snooping around his personal space.
Mock family and tradition.
Always put your needs first.
Always hide your tears.
Forget special occasions.
Be aggressive when you argue.
Invite strangers into your home.
Hesitate following through on a decision when he's unsure.
Let out a wild side when you hit forty.
Become cynical with age and lose all hope.
Let your home-life become totally unstructured.

EARTHLY BLISS (AKA SEX)

There's something funny about the Cancer man's view of conjugal sex. Somehow, once you establish a home together, and especially if you become parents, your Crab's notion of sex doesn't quite jibe with the woman who increasingly embodies the figure of "Mother." As time rolls by, he may lose interest in sex . . . with you, *not* because he doesn't love you, but maybe because he loves you too much and feels you're too good and wholesome to engage in such "vulgarity." That's why you want to keep the sex tender and nurturing, and never let it become really hard or loud.

Sometimes the Cancer man needs to exploit his rich imagination in order to continue having good sex. Maybe he delights in inventing new and fantastic love scenarios. Or maybe he has to imagine you're someone less worthy than his dear wife (though he won't admit it). Imagination, emotions, and moods will always play a big role in sex, so don't expect it to be a straightforward, primitive affair. You'll have to know how to please him without being crude.

This moody creature will keep you guessing. And you won't always know what works. Just don't let the mother complex get the better of him and ruin what could be a fantastic love life. Make him realize that you are first and foremost a *woman,* and that a good sex life can only strengthen your bond.

AND CHEATING . . . ?

You normally won't have to worry about your Crab husband cheating just for the sake of it, and he's not the type to actively seek out extramarital fun, but the way he deals (or cannot deal) with his mother complex may play a role in his future loyalty. If he doesn't mature with age and begins to see you as this holier-than-thou mother figure, he might feel increasingly guilty about having sex with you, or even about the kind of sex he would *like* to have. And this is when he could get involved in a clandestine affair, with someone he can treat more as a sex object.

Then there's always the "neglected child" scenario. If your Cancer husband is not getting the attention he needs, or if you prove too weak and undisciplined to give him the sense of structure and protection he craves, he could go looking for another "mom."

Unless you are highly intuitive, chances are you may never know about such illicit activity, since the Crab is both secretive and clever. On the other hand, if his true motive is avenging your lack of compassion and love, he might purposely leave traces so you discover his naughty behavior. (And yes, he'll want to be punished and grounded for a week.)

The Crab is a complex, often difficult, creature to deal with, but if you know how to handle with him, he shouldn't have any reason to deceive you.

REASONS HE MIGHT CHEAT

- If he needs to unleash his sexuality on less worthy women
- If he feels neglected and unloved
- If he meets a better "mom"
- If you can't understand his more complicated needs
- If the full moon draws out his romantic and irrational behavior

WHAT YOU CAN DO

- Appeal to his fear of insecurity by pointing out cheating husbands who lost their house, family, and friends.

- Keep a long leash on him.
- Encourage him to write (instead of act) out his secret desires.
- Encourage him to live vicariously through epic film and drama.
- Make your body language show the disdain you feel for unfaithful, "weak" men (and cheap women).
- Let him know that cheating is the *one* thing you do not accept.

SOME THINGS TO TWEAK

Even when he *finally* grows up, the Crab remains hypersensitive, taking insult to even the slightest negative remark or gesture (and sometimes to even imagined ones). The result is often a crabby guy who retreats back into his protective shell and is no fun to be around. You'd do him a huge favor by (gently) making him aware of this self-defeating tendency, and helping him overcome it. Maybe you could enroll him in a martial arts class (Crabs actually thrive in such activities), or get him to start an aggressive sport. Once he begins to feel tougher on the outside, he may feel tougher on the inside (and be a happier person for it).

It would also be constructive to help him find an outlet for his overactive imagination. The Crab has such a need for dreaming, which might make his life and relationships messy. Try encouraging him to read, write, paint, or play an instrument. If you don't help him to cultivate a creative hobby, he could turn to drinking instead (the potential is very real). Let him know it's okay to dream and fantasize as long as he continues to take his everyday responsibilities seriously. He'll accept positive advice as long as you present it in a mature and loving way. Just don't criticize him.

AND HAPPILY EVER AFTER . . .

A lifetime with a Cancer man will have its ups and downs, but at least things won't get too routine and stale. And you'll definitely have practice honing your woman's (mother's) intuition just figuring out what he wants and what he needs. It might even be fun switching back and forth from wife to mommy. In any case, you have many challenges to look forward to—and some unreasonable behavior, too. Still, you have to accept your Crab the way he is, even when he's testing you, because what he really wants is that one thing only a mother can give: unconditional love. Yes, he seems complex, but the key to his happiness is more simple than you think.

Leo, the Lion

(about July 23 till about August 22)

So you want to date the king of the jungle? Well, who wouldn't want the attention of this superior beast? There's just one problem: He knows he's great, and you'll have to be noble enough yourself to even attract his notice, let alone lure him into a full-fledged relationship. His standards are high, due to his innate nobility and utter idealism, and he's probably one of the hardest men to impress.

The Leo man is in love with the idea of love, but the kind of woman he desires doesn't come along often. And it's okay, because he can go solo for a long time (though he can't go long without sex). He loves females, but does not *have* to have a steady partner to be happy. Still, he has so much warmth and love to offer the woman who merits these gifts. He just needs to find the right one, not only for romance, but for the role of mother to his future brood, so sooner or later he'll have to make his choice and settle down.

The Leo man tends to admire star-type girls, those who are beautiful or rich or successful (as long as they don't outshine him). In fact, he seeks the woman who will reflect his glory while being able to maintain her own identity. She has to know how to dress, how to entertain, and how to make him look good. At the same time, she has to be mature enough to be able to be a good mother later on. And, most important, she needs to understand the balance of power and the fact that there isn't room for two kings.

If you aren't intimidated yet, keep hanging in there because wonderful things await the girl who catches this man's heart. The Leo man in love is generous and affectionate, the type who will shower his lioness with physical tenderness, as well as expensive gifts and jewelry (or whatever is "lavish" for his personal budget). This is the guy you see in the movies who comes home with a little velvet box from Harry Winston's, for no special reason (have you ever wondered why you've never met one of those guys?). Yes, he loves to spoil his sweetheart, but be aware that his motives are not purely romantic. He knows a beautifully decorated girlfriend or wife only reflects his own success, which elicits envy from others. In fact, the Leo man is in search of a trophy wife because, between us, he loves to brag and show off. But he's so damn loyal and lovable and fun that you just have to forgive him for it!

The single Lion is not a homebody, content to pass his nights in front of the TV. (Even when he is married and has little cubs running around, he *still* loves a great party.) He wants to be *seen*—at the hottest restaurants, the best parties, and the most exclusive events—preferably with a fantastic girl on his arm. What he really seeks is an audience, though he doesn't always elicit its sympathy, probably because the way he enters a room is already annoying to some, who take his regal posture for arrogance and conceit. Wonder who that guy in the circle is, dominating the conversation and cutting everyone else off? Yup, that's your Lion, convinced that he is the most fascinating and superior man in the room—and he usually is!

Luckily, there's another breed of Lion as well, one that is all sun and warmth. He's the most popular guy in town, the type who knows how to keep his superiority complex in check and make everyone feel good. Both men and women idolize this Lion, and secretly want to be (or bed) him. His warm energy can light up even the dullest of parties, so no wise person would dare keep him off the invitation list. This type of Lion is more reasonable in his dating standards and has more successful relationships.

No matter what type of Leo man, though, the fact remains that he thrives in positions of authority. A clever woman will sympathize with his raw needs instead of fighting for power. And a *very* clever woman will make him feel like he's the boss calling all the shots when, in reality, it's she who ends up getting her way in the end. (Some Lions are happy enough being the figurehead.) There's really no reason to challenge him or strike a blow to his ego, because he has good intentions and a noble heart. Besides, you'd hurt this big cat more than you think—he might let out a ferocious roar, but he'd sulk back to his lair to lick his wounds when nobody's watching. Feel sorry for him? Then indulge him in love, pampering, and passionate sex so he can reassume his position in the jungle.

THE LEO MAN IS

AT BEST	AT WORST
Dignified	Egocentric
Noble	Vain
Creative	Proud
Affectionate	Domineering
Loyal	Inflexible
Generous	Arrogant
Organized	Condescending
Idealistic	Authoritative
Warm	Hedonistic
Confident	Extravagant
Influential	Self-Indulgent
Powerful	Cold
Determined	Power-Hungry
Entertaining	Fierce
Playful	Brutal

What it really comes down to is this: The Leo man just wants to be loved and admired and respected. And that means making him feel like a king. And giving him the physical affection he craves. And praising his unique feats (however mediocre they are in reality), whether they be athletic, creative, or professional. This Lion needs to be fully appreciated for the great beast he is and will cherish the woman who can recognize and applaud his talents and accomplishments.

The Leo man is great in bed, successful in his career, and respected in society. Who could ask for more? If you are willing to let him reign on his hill under the sun (his natural "right"), you might very well become his lioness. Too much? Maybe for some gals out there. The Lion demands and expects much more than most other men of the zodiac. But he gives much more in return.

SOME FAMOUS LEO MEN

Bill Clinton, Robert Redford, Arnold Schwarzenegger, Ben Affleck, Edward Norton, Antonio Banderas, Sean Penn, Larry Ellison, Billy Bob Thornton, Robert De Niro, Pete Sampras, Fidel Castro, Napoléon, Mick Jagger, Carl Jung, Benito Mussolini, Henry Ford, Neil Armstrong, Andy Warhol, "Magic" Johnson, Kevin Spacey, Steve Martin, Yves St.-Laurent

MUST HAVE BEEN A LEO MAN

Cal Hockley *(Titanic)* (okay, one of the more arrogant Lions)

THE SEDUCTION

To capture this beast's attention, you'll need to rise high above mediocrity. The first step is making yourself believe you're someone special. Once you begin to believe it, others will begin to believe it, too. Start by learning perfect posture, poise, and how to make great entrances. And know how to dress. You want this big cat to think he's found the puuur-fect match!

From there on, let this Lion take the lead so he can show off his romantic finesse. And don't hide that sparkle in your eye—the Lion wants to know you find him irresistible. Just make sure you keep your standards high—that means declining last-minute dates or after-hours meetings. No matter how attractive he is, you must stand by your principles.

Once the romance begins, expect the royal treatment—flowers, presents, dinners, parties, etc. Just be sure to dress the part so he can show you off to the world. Most important, treat him with respect, in private and (especially) in public. To him, the world is like a stage and he wants top billing.

After establishing some kind of bond, let passion take its course and give in to his seduction. (A slap in the face or standoffish behavior means good-bye forever.) It might be romantic, dramatic, or even very natural, but the seduction is crucial to this imaginative, passionate beast. Play along with it, let yourself go, and indulge in great sex. And pray the chemistry is *real* (you'll both know soon enough). The Lion won't settle for just any female—he has too many choices.

SEX

passionate, ardent, noble, frequent

Sex is always a big issue with the Leo man. It makes him feel powerful. It makes him feel sexy. It makes him feel loved. And it feels great, too. But truly great sex means mutual passion, so even the most seemingly "perfect" female won't last long if she turns out to be a cold fish in bed.

The right female for him will be the one he can create fireworks with. And not just once a month. This beast has a real appetite and needs to be satisfied regularly and thoroughly. Still, romance and seduction are important to him and should continue to play a role in lovemaking. And the right female will know how to entice him with beautiful lingerie and appetizing body language.

No matter how dramatic the Lion is, sex should stay noble and decent (unless it's a casual or one-time deal). He just couldn't admire a woman who would do *anything* to please him, especially if it's degrading or pathetic. No matter how many women he's had, this man is still an idealist at heart and wants sex to stay beautiful.

DOS AND DON'TS OF A GREAT RELATIONSHIP

DO

Have a great sense of style.
Know how to make others admire you.
Appreciate the arts.
Have a taste for the finer things.
Behave with dignity and class.
Shower him with praise.
Put him on a pedestal.
Have character and principles.
Love children.
Have hobbies and areas of special interest.
Enjoy parties and entertaining.
Have respectable and influential friends.
Be creative, if possible.
Be supple enough to accommodate his needs.
Praise his accomplishments, big or small.

Be petty or small.
Be frigid or cold.
Treat him with disrespect.
Challenge his authority beyond reason.
Try to outshine him.
Let yourself go.
Be inactive and lazy.
Ruin his day with your negative energy.
Do things that put your reputation at risk.
Make him jealous or suspicious.
Be sloppy and unattractive.
Hurt his ego.
Ever criticize his children (if he has any).
Make him feel unimportant and unloved.
Compare him to others in your circle (unless it's to make him look good).

BEST WAYS TO IMPRESS

Throw the best parties in town.
Be among the Rich, Young, and Beautiful crowd.
Be a fashion editor at *Vogue*.
Be a famous artist (singer, dancer, actress, fashion designer).
Have a beautiful and unique rapport with children.

BEST WAYS TO GET DUMPED

Have an affair with his best friend (you'll both get dumped).
Humiliate him in public.
Be mean to a child (especially his).
Be nice to one of his "enemies."
Be a model of mediocrity.

FASHION

Finally, a man who loves to shop! The Leo man adores clothes and the women who know how to wear them, so those who view clothes as mere material worn to cover the body won't score big points with this guy. To him, fashion is not just a way of expressing oneself, it's also about style and image. Even a plain-looking female can empower herself with a beautiful wardrobe.

Some Lions love glamour, others love pure class, but most like a mix of the two, resulting in a look that elicits admiration (and envy) from others. Even workout clothes should display flair, and there's *never* a good excuse for getting caught outdoors in a dirty old T-shirt and raggedy flip-flops. Yes, dressing for a Leo man costs time and money, but he's worth it, isn't he? (He certainly thinks so.)

Unfortunately, it doesn't stop at the thread. As if a great wardrobe weren't expensive enough, there're the extras to think about: real jewelry, beautiful watches, big movie-star sunglasses, the latest shoes and handbags (let's not even get into the pampering beauty treatments). And skill and a good eye are crucial in blending everything together to make an outfit "work." If in doubt, check out the latest issue of your favorite fashion magazine so you don't go making a blunder—your Lion would barely forgive you.

GIFT IDEAS: Those that are royal, luxurious, exclusive, or leisurely

BEER BUDGET

One-hour massage (your hands)
Red, orange, or yellow swim trunks (he likes sunny colors)
Beautiful designer tie
Two champagne glasses (his and yours)
Sunglasses
Monogrammed shirt

CHAMPAGNE BUDGET

Designer briefcase
Latest video camera
Box of Cuban cigars (if he smokes)
Certificate to upscale spa
Luxury car
Deluxe vacation

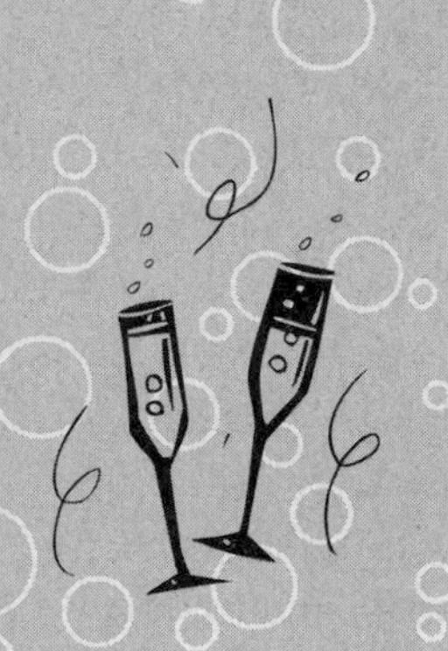

ADD SOME SPICE

The Leo man tends to like things the way they are, but there's no doubt the right spice here and there could add some tasteful drama.

Some Ideas

1. Get back into an old artistic hobby (e.g., piano, dancing, opera set design) so he's *vying* for your free time.
2. Go to an important party and be the most attractive woman there.
3. Get into a dramatic fight, then make up with passionate love.
4. Bet on something, then let the winner demand his *any* wish.

IF YOU SENSE A LOOMING BREAKUP

The Leo man won't waste time with the wrong girl. When a relationship isn't fulfilling his ideals, it's just a matter of time before he makes an honest break. And it won't be hard to know when his heart's growing heavy—though he's a good actor, the Leo man can't fake love.

Danger Signs to Watch For

- Growing indifference and coldness
- Increasing selfishness
- Increasing stubbornness
- More nights out with the boys

If you can't bear even the thought of him leaving you, get your act together now before it's too late. Think about inviting him out to dinner for once—and *not* at McDonald's. Wear your most stunning outfit and talk over candlelight. After a few glasses of wine, the Lion might just spill his heart. If you're lucky, the obstacles to a beautiful relationship won't be insurmountable. But if the problems are fundamental and permanent, there's not much use in thinking you can change his stubborn mind.

In the worst-case scenario of him saying good-bye, be sure that you stand tall and dignified. This is not the man you want to humiliate with a glass of water in the face or some other hysterical gesture. And vindictive behavior won't be appreciated. You want to be the bigger person in the end, so let him end it if he wants. Just keep your poise and smile. The Leo man is another one who could eventually end up with an ex-girlfriend, and the chances are all the greater if the breakup was "all class."

In the meantime, go on with your big plans in life, and should you hear about it, don't let his flirting and dating kill you—he's just looking for a boost to his morale. The only hope for a woman hooked on a Lion is to make a fabulous comeback in the future, and to display behavior that intensifies the qualities he loved in her in the first place and eradicates those he disliked. And it wouldn't hurt to be seen around town with a very eligible bachelor (even if he is just a friend). You can bet your Lion is keeping tabs on you, and if you play it right, he could come back roaring to reclaim his Lioness.

AND NEVER FORGET

His essential need to shine

HOW MR. LEO SEES YOU

	AT BEST	AT WORST
Aries	dynamic, ambitious	competitive, bossy
Taurus	affectionate, loyal	jealous, stubborn
Gemini	supple, youthful	undependable, insincere
Cancer	romantic, pampering	negative, disorganized
Leo	noble, passionate	challenging, unyielding
Virgo	neat, organized	critical, inhibited
Libra	accommodating, tasteful	vacillating, flirtatious
Scorpio	intense, magnetic	manipulative, controlling
Sagittarius	optimistic, fun	informal, meandering
Capricorn	ambitious, loyal	unaffectionate, harsh
Aquarius	sociable, eye-catching	unreliable, cool
Pisces	compassionate, artistic	negligent, dishonest

BEST BETS	WHY NOT?	CHALLENGING
Libra	Aries	Aquarius
Gemini	Virgo	Capricorn
Cancer	Scorpio	
Leo	Sagittarius	
Taurus	Pisces	

LEO MAN (Bill Clinton) and SCORPIO WOMAN (Hillary Rodham Clinton)

Talk about a power couple! The strong combination of Leo man/Scorpio woman has great potential, though there can be lots of fireworks. It's also a long-term coupling, both signs having the ability to aim for lasting goals. The Leo man just has to be careful about putting his needs first, and always seeking an audience to impress. Sure, it's great to feel loved and admired in public life, but the private life should never be neglected, especially when one is hooked up with a possessive Scorpio woman! On her side, a Scorpio woman can work well behind the scenes and be the pillar of strength in difficult times. And if she can rise above her darker side and focus her intense energy on her husband's or her own career (which obviously benefits her precious children), this couple can go a *long* way. Of course, there will be moments when the Scorpio woman extinguishes the Leo's fire, and lots of "power" struggles (these are two big egos!), but the pairing of these two signs has what it takes to achieve big things, as well as survive almost any crisis. On the other hand, if these two passionate creatures can't stop sparring, an ugly breakup is almost inevitable.

SOME ADVICE—TAKE IT OR LEAVE IT

YOUR SIGN	
Aries	DO: focus your passion on *him* DON'T: try to be the boss and call all the shots
Taurus	DO: endear yourself to him with your warm physical affection (and great massages!) DON'T: refuse to budge when his demands are within reason
Gemini	DO: focus on conversation topics that he enjoys DON'T: display your tendency to flirt with other men
Cancer	DO: make him the hero of your romantic fairy tale DON'T: alienate him with your murky moods
Leo	DO: show off your flair for entertaining DON'T: try to be the big boss
Virgo	DO: use your efficiency to help him succeed DON'T: nag and criticize him
Libra	DO: show off your fashion and social savvy DON'T: be light and airy when he craves some fire
Scorpio	DO: entrap him with your undying passion DON'T: sting him in his weak spots
Sagittarius	DO: delight him with your enthusiasm for life DON'T: become too casual in behavior or dress
Capricorn	DO: let him know you can make him a great man DON'T: keep up your cold front
Aquarius	DO: have friends and hobbies that fit with his DON'T: act so independently that you make him feel unimportant
Pisces	DO: cultivate your creative streak and stick to your projects DON'T: ever let him doubt your faithfulness

Looking Farther Down the Road

THE ENGAGEMENT

A Lion in love is a lion who has already fantasized about a grandiose method of proposal. And if he's in the stage of life where he feels ready to settle down, you can be quite sure that a proposal will come as long as you continue to maintain his "ideal." Still, even one gross blunder on your part can make two years of perfect dating obsolete, so don't blow it now that you've finally gained his respect and exclusive love. The Lion considers getting married a terribly noble deed, and he must be convinced that you can live up to his terribly high expectations.

You'll know he's thinking marriage when he starts talking about kids or begins gazing at little babies in the park. But if he's taking too long, you can always mention that the Big Shot is calling again, making it clear that he's finally ready to settle down. If your boyfriend is truly worthy of the Lion title, he'll solidify his position as King of your Heart in no time.

THE WEDDING

Don't you dare think about economizing for this big day! Your Leo fiancé expects a royal wedding (or as "royal" as your budget permits), not a second-rate act. Feel free to consult His Royal Highness on wedding details—he has great ideas and would love to share them with you. Just don't give him the idea that you're a zero in the planning department—his future Lioness must have party know-how.

Of course, he'll want his wedding to be the talk of the town, so keep up the facade (even if it'll drive you to bankruptcy!).

This event is not only about love and commitment, it's about public image, so don't let your Lionheart down. And pay special attention to your wedding dress. Of course, getting Valentino to design it would be the crowning achievement, but since most of us are mere mortals, finding the perfect dress that conveys beauty and class will be enough to endear you to your Lion. Just don't neglect your bridesmaids—even they need to be worthy of the honor (and they'll love you for offering a dress they can actually be proud of!).

THE HONEYMOON

If there's one thing a Lion loves more than parties, it's vacations! Especially the grandiose (even decadent) ones, where time stands still and pricetags don't count. If there's ever a time in your life when you indulge in a splendid trip, let it be this one. That means first-rate hotels, special treatment, and enough stylish outfits to see you through to the end. And don't forget to schedule his-and-her massages into a busy agenda so your Lion gets his due pampering. (Yes, you probably spoil him enough already, but he would surely decline to agree.) Your Lion wants to feel *special,* so don't disappoint him now that you're married.

And yet it's not just about the luxuries and special treatment—it's also about this idealistic thing called *love.* Now, more than ever, is the time to show your Lion how thrilled you are to be his wife. And you can never be too affectionate, devoted, and attracted to this beast—in fact, he thinks it's perfectly normal. So don't disillusion him with cold or indifferent behavior, especially on this significant trip. This Lion wants to be the center of your universe, now and forever after.

Honeymoon Sex

Yes, the sex has to be passionate and wonderful and spectacular and all the rest. And totally uninhibited. But noble, too. There's nothing wrong with making love in total and pure abandon as long as it stays decent. To keep sex a first-rate production, make sure you have tons of silk nighties and floral panties and flirty bras. And don't go for the no-makeup look, even between the sheets. Dress the role of an A-list star and make love like the heroine of a romantic drama.

MAKING IT IN THE LONG HAUL

The future looks quite bright through your Lion's eyes. As long as everything goes his way, he should remain content. But any problems of the heart will bring gloomy days, so misunderstandings and quarrels should be sorted out as soon as possible. Also, questions of power and authority could bring eventual difficulties if someone's ego evolves throughout the marriage (yours, namely), so avoid drastic behavior that could bring out the beast in him.

DOS AND DON'TS FOR LASTING BLISS

DO

Remain loyal and devoted.
Engage in activities that will allow him to "shine."
Continue to improve your entertaining skills.
Stay well-groomed and presentable.
Nurse him back to happiness when he's suffered a blow.
Take up some sort of artistic or creative hobby.
Show him how much you love him (all the time).
Applaud his career victories, big and small.

Turn your home into a royal Lion's den.
Surprise him from time to time with presents and toys.
Take frequent romantic vacations.
Fill your agenda with fun activities and events.
Get dressed up and be seen at exclusive restaurants.
Serve him a royal breakfast in bed once a week.
Make time for lazy days (sleeping in, morning sex, lounging around in silk pajamas, reading newspapers, indulging in massages, etc.).

Become cynical or gloomy with age.
Become boring and disinterested as years roll by.
Make him feel less important as time goes by.
Make him feel threatened if your career bolts past his.
Show interest in other attractive men.
Go to the supermarket in sweats and rollers.
Do anything that could shame your Lion in public.
Make him believe you're not fit to become a mother.
Criticize him in public—*ever*!
Mock his latest hobby (however silly it is).
Tell him that he can't afford the new suit he's dying for.
Neglect your home and garden.
Threaten him and give nasty ultimatums.
Let him get away with unreasonably selfish behavior (sometimes you have to put your foot down).

EARTHLY BLISS (AKA SEX)

Great sex is a major ingredient in the recipe of a successful marriage. And the Lion certainly has a healthy appetite, so make sure you are willing and able to satiate it, even as you head into middle age. Being innately creative, your Lion husband may come up with new ideas to keep the sex dramatic and fun, so play along if you want to keep him smiling. And *never* make the mistake of making him feel unattractive, even as he approaches his hundredth birthday. Let him know that sex with him is king.

Still, you don't want to experiment with obscene acts, because the Leo man usually maintains high principles in the sex department, especially with his wife and the mother of his cubs. Sex should always be passionate, fun, and sometimes dramatic, but let him play out his more beastly scenes in his dreams. And if he wants you to show your satisfaction by screaming or grunting or making a lot of noise, that's fine. Just don't put yourself in compromising positions that could deflate his respect for you.

AND CHEATING . . . ?

What an undignified topic! The moment you and your Leo man exchanged wedding bands was the moment he vowed fidelity, which is crucial to his idealistic vision of marriage. Besides, a Leo husband takes his responsibilities seriously, so he might find it shameful to cheat even if he meets an amazing woman. Still, he does have animal instincts, and even the best of Lions can go astray.

The biggest danger is if he meets an extraordinary creature, one who knows how to make him feel attractive and kingly. Even if he manages to control himself, he could fantasize about wining, dining, and bedding her. And after the first goof you make, like harmlessly flirting with an attractive man or siding with his employee in a dispute, he could find reason to "justify" his actions and turn his fantasies into reality. In the end, though, he would feel guilty and miserable, especially when he realizes that you do, indeed, adore him. And then he would try everything in his power to make it up to you (even if you never knew in the first place).

Some of the more hedonistic or artistic Leo men are less loyal because they find it harder to resist fresh romance and sex. And they find it a pity to limit their greatness to just one woman. If you are married to this type of Lion, you'll have to keep tabs on him to make sure he doesn't go hunting. But at least let him flirt so he can enjoy some feminine attention other than yours. If you're lucky, that will be enough to keep him happy.

It won't be easy for a Leo man to hide an affair, because his attitude says so much. And because he's not the most discreet person, it wouldn't be long before a friend of yours spots him impressing another female. Still, don't torture yourself with what-ifs. The principled Lion hates shabby behavior and shouldn't betray you unless you give him great reason to.

REASONS HE MIGHT CHEAT

- If you make him feel unloved and unappreciated
- If you don't treat him with the respect he demands
- If the beast gets the better of him
- If there's no more romance in your marriage
- If your sex life is unsatisfying

WHAT YOU CAN DO

- Show him how much you love him (regularly).
- Tell him you admire his loyalty and class.
- Treat him with *respect.*
- Keep your sex life great.
- Make him so proud of you that he's scared to ever lose you.
- Let him know that cheating is a sign of great weakness (and that any bozo could do it).

SOME THINGS TO TWEAK

The unyielding Lion sees no reason to change, but as your relationship deepens, you might want to help him out in some potential problem areas, as long as you never seem patronizing or condescending. The Lion is a proud animal and dreads being in a position where he has to "stoop" down, but this attitude can result in poor decisions and lost opportunities. Try making him understand that asking for help or forgiveness or some other "petty" deed is not so bad, and can even help make him a bigger man in the end. Of course, he won't want to believe you, but he might think back to your words after a pride-motivated action ends up costing him a lot (like a job or a friendship). Sure, a healthy dose of pride is good for everyone, but not when it gets in the way of good sense and self-evolution.

Then it would also be nice if the Lion would grow up and stop expecting special treatment. This man often assumes his throne in the household (or wherever else) and expects everyone else to do the dirty work (including you). Assure him that he is, indeed, special and deserves respect, but sooner or later you'll have to break the news to him that others deserve respect, too. Besides, he should know by now that truly great men never have big ideas of themselves—the greater they are, the more humble they can be. Get him to join you (and others) in some menial tasks and encourage him to get on his hands and knees from time to time—it could lead to a changed man.

AND HAPPILY EVER AFTER . . .

The sun should shine on your future with Mr. Leo if you turn out to be the ideal partner—that means being Super Wife, Mother, Woman, and Hostess, or, simply put, fit for a king. And you'll be happy to know that as your bond grows deeper, your Leo man might actually forgive some of your imperfections, too. Just go on having a fun and romantic life together while maintaining your principles (and living up to his), and continue to make him feel special and loved. Yes, you might sometimes feel like you're living with a spoiled brat (or, worse, a dictator), but this man has a big heart deep down inside, one he's more than eager to share with the right woman.

Virgo, the Virgin

(about August 23 till about September 22)

The Virgo man is made for the sensible girl. This neat, practical, and dependable person has a no-nonsense approach to romance that will delight the modern girl with a busy agenda. Like the Virgin, he's not too sophisticated in affairs of the heart, but his clean, honest outlook on life makes him a good candidate for a wholesome relationship.

This man might present a picture of calm, but the truth is that he's quite nervous inside. Maybe this is why he so easily develops habits—they help channel his inner anxiety. It might also be why he loves to classify and organize everything, as order brings calm to his nerves. It may even be to blame for his slight hypochondria. The Virgin is the first to race to the doctor (or spend hours on the Internet doing medical research) the minute he feels a twinge in his stomach. Likewise, this man will usually have an above-average interest in health, natural medicine, and fitness, and an obvious disdain for any female who abuses her mind or body. A man of moderation, he's not always the life of the party, but at least he can drive everyone home safely!

The Virgin has a tendency to be a prude, but this doesn't mean he doesn't enjoy women and sex. He just hates vulgarity, overt sexuality, and even public displays of affection. However, at the same time, he has a slightly naughty side that may surprise his acquaintances. Still, sex is probably not top priority with this man (unless it happens to be one of his "habits," in which case he can become particularly obsessive about it). But he might *think* about it a lot.

This is why some girls find him so attractive. Because he doesn't approach you with his tongue hanging out, he exudes a sort of standoffish or untouchable quality that drives some women crazy. And he just appears to be someone who really has it "together," even though this isn't always the reality. In any case, he presents a real challenge for girls who are used to more primitive types, and you can bet that he takes pleasure in being one of the more "difficult cases."

The discriminating Virgo man is usually attracted to nice-smelling, well-groomed, successful girls who have a good head on their shoulders and a winning personality. And there has to be a good intellectual rapport between them. Ruled by his head, the Virgin is not impressed with flamboyant, dramatic, or wild women. He respects those who live in a rational world where everything makes sense. At the same time, there is often an element of "interest" involved in his choice of girlfriend. It's not really a "What's in it for me?" type of thing. But there's no denying that the Virgo man is talented at making sensible, logical decisions, ones that often end up serving his best interests, even in matters of the heart.

Unfairly, the Virgo man has acquired the reputation for being boring. Not true! The Virgin can be one of the most fun men around—you just have to know him well enough. He enjoys gossip and can bring you to tears with his uncanny yet humorous criticisms of people and situations. This is the man who can spend hours after a dinner party discussing and analyzing the guests' attitudes, charades, motives, and outfits (though he sometimes misjudges the more complex people). And he always has an astute comment to make about any situation or development. Intelligent girls should never pass a dull moment with the Virgin.

A girl interested in capturing a Virgo heart must be warned that he is one of the men most likely to stay single. Many a bachelor is born under this sign, but don't think it's because he's against marriage. The Virgin simply finds it difficult to cohabit with another person because he's a clean freak who can't stand seeing his organized habitat turned into total disarray. (A clever girl will stay at her own pad until she's married.) This is the guy who will bicker over different methods of rolling toothpaste tubes or organizing CDs. What? Doesn't sound very sexy? Well, some of the most attractive men alive are born under the sign of Virgo (see below). You just have to look past his annoying habits to fully appreciate him as a man. And as for his famous tendency to nag and criticize—it's just part of his character. Either give him nothing to complain about or learn to live with it. Eventually, he'll recognize that he's not perfect himself and may even forgive you your foibles.

And yet it's hard for him to forgive careless and costly behavior. The Virgo man *hates* waste, especially in the money department. If your eyes are set on him as a potential romantic interest, don't let him know you're a shopping fiend, or that you have a drawer full of unpaid parking tickets and compounding penalty fees. And don't offer to go Dutch unless you really want to split the bill—he'll be more than happy to oblige.

Because the Virgin is fundamentally insecure, he'll be suspicious of any woman who likes him, overanalyzing every conversation in his head until he gets sick. What does she see in me? Why is she with me? What are her true motives? Only

THE VIRGO MAN IS

AT BEST	AT WORST
Practical	Critical
Discriminating	Anxious
Analytical	Carping
Logical	Cheap
Rational	Insecure
Efficient	Unromantic
Health-Conscious	Cynical
Intelligent	Prudish
Hygienic	Petty
Modest	Dissatisfied
Technical	Timid
Useful	Self-Serving
Orderly	Anal-Retentive
Reasonable	Dull
Helpful	Hypochondriacal

your constancy, reliability, and loyalty, proven over a period of time, will convince him that he is truly loved. And that is when he will finally loosen up and be able to enjoy your time together.

But never count on grandiose expressions of love, either in public or private, because it's just not part of his nature. Aware of his inability to say or do the right things, he is not comfortable in romantic situations, and when he senses it's time to make a move, he may even develop some sort of complex. This is why the Virgo man is often seduced by aggressive women, those who take the initiative and lead the way. But "aggressive" does not mean "fast," which conjures up images of unhygienic promiscuity and sexual diseases (yuck!). In this case, "aggressive" means confident and strong.

Although it takes a while, a Virgo man will eventually open up to his sweetheart and convince himself that he actually might be experiencing this mysterious thing called "love." And once he is yours, he won't disappoint you. The Virgin may not be the romantic type to shower you with flowers, or the sentimental type who remembers every special anniversary, but he will compensate for this with an earthy practicality and the ability to get those bills paid!

SOME FAMOUS VIRGO MEN

Richard Gere, Sean Conner, Colin Firth, Hugh Grant, Keanu Reeves, David Duchovny, Warren Buffet, Tommy Lee Jones, Ryan Phillippe, Oliver Stone, Michael Jackson, Jimmy Connors, Charlie Sheen, Bob Newhart, Leo Tolstoy, Stephen King, Prince Harry Windsor

MUST HAVE BEEN A VIRGO MAN

Mark Darcy *(Bridget Jones's Diary)*

THE SEDUCTION

Getting the busy Virgo man to notice you will be a big enough challenge. This man has little time for diversion, and it takes more than "one sighting" to pique his interest. The best scenario for meeting him is in the workplace, or somewhere else where he spends a lot of time (for example, the health club), so he can see how you operate on a day-to-day basis. But if you happen to meet him at a cocktail or dinner party, impress him quickly before he heads for home. That means decent behavior, interesting conversation, and a winning smile.

The Virgo man refuses to make a fool of himself, even if it means letting a potential love interest escape from his grasp. He must be certain there's some mutual interest before taking the risk of asking you out, so don't play games and pretend you have a million more interesting things to do than go to lunch with him if that's what you really want.

As you get to know each other, establish a good intellectual rapport that stimulates him and makes him want more of your company. And don't stop there—flirt a bit if you want (but only in a clever way), and indulge in some subtle but suggestive body language, the kind that sets his mind abuzz (as in: Was that an accident, or did she purposely brush my arm?). The Virgo man actually admires females who are confident enough to take the lead, as long as they're discreet about it at the same time.

After a natural rapport has been established, it's time for the next step. Try encouraging the advance he's been thinking about making, maybe after a great movie or fantastic discussion—but never in a public spot. Let the seduction play out at his place, where he feels most comfortable. (But make a pre-seduction trip to the ladies' room to make sure a big piece of spinach isn't stuck between your teeth.) If anything goes wrong in bed, don't talk about it (or just pretend it didn't happen). Otherwise he could get some sort of a complex or decide you're no good together. Give him time to figure out what makes you tick so the next time is perfect.

SEX

clean, technically good, safe

The Virgo man enjoys good sex, but not just with anyone. And not too many girls out there can excite him. Unless a female is really worth his time, he has better things to do than get hot and sweaty between the sheets. But when he's with a woman he really admires, he can get a lot of satisfaction in bed (unless he discovers that she's dirty or unhygienic).

Still, he's not exceptionally passionate in bed, because he's not a passionate guy in general. And he's not ruled by his emotions, anyway. So don't worry if he doesn't scream out in a frenzy—it doesn't (usually) mean he's bored. Your Virgo lover is probably just concentrating on his work.

As he gets used to you, the Virgin might start letting go. And he might stop analyzing sex and just start feeling it. It would be great of you to praise his performance, just to give him that little boost of confidence. But never make the mistake of comparing him to previous boyfriends, even if it's meant as a compliment—he wouldn't like the feeling of being critiqued on his bedroom skills.

DOS AND DON'TS OF A GREAT RELATIONSHIP

DO

Be clean and hygienic.
Have self-confidence.
Have a sparkling personality.
Set up ambitious (but not foolish) goals.
Spend money wisely.
Spend your free time on productive activities.
Watch your eating habits (and his).
Have a rigorous exercise regimen.
Be well-read and informed.
Enjoy gossip and discussions.
Be up-to-date on computer skills.
Give him a boost of confidence.
Brighten his day with a smile.
Know when to take the initiative.
Know how to make decisions.

DON'T

Talk or behave in a vulgar way.
Smoke, do drugs, or drink too much.
Demand PDA (Public Display of Affection).
Criticize him (that's his department).
Be flamboyant or bizarre.
Make a mess of his car or personal space.
Be overly emotional and irrational.

Take stupid risks.
Attempt kinky or strange sex (unless he asks for it, which is highly unlikely).
Depend on him to get your life in order.
Become lazy, physically or mentally.
Lie to or deceive him.
Make unreasonable demands.
Be extravagant or wasteful.
Ask him to lend you money.
Try to take up all his free time.

BEST WAYS TO IMPRESS

Be a successful CEO.
Know how to make your own clothes.
Be a medical doctor, ready to cater to his every health concern.
Have a live-in housekeeper.
Just be perfect (it's that easy).

BEST WAYS TO GET DUMPED

Get sloppy drunk and vomit all over his brand-new sofa (he'll probably stick you with the cleaning bill, too).
Be drowning in debt (and ask him to pitch in).
Brag about how strong your immune system must be now that you've had every venereal disease in the book.
Walk around his apartment naked.
Attack him in a psycho PMS fit.

FASHION

There is a Virgo man who is "in the know" of the current trends, just because he tends to be well-informed. But most Virgins don't care much for fashion, especially if (or maybe because) it encourages frivolous expenditures and waste. (Shoes and handbags for each season? Not if *he's* paying!) A well-groomed, sensible look is more important than the latest hemline, so classic but pretty clothes work better than trendy ones.

Maybe more important is using good sense when dressing. Ideally, there should be some underlying logic in the way you choose to mix and match your pieces, and your outfits should correspond to your figure—the criticizing Virgo man will be wondering, for example, why you wear body-hugging clothing if it makes you look six months pregnant. For the same reason, impractical clothes that are impossible to move around in won't work. The best bet is to dress for the occasion (whether that calls for discretion, femininity, or glamour) and always look neat and presentable.

Accessories are best kept to a minimum. Even if you're exceptionally talented at creating a complex look that works, too many belts and purses and earrings and stockings might unnerve him. If there's one piece you should show off, it's a great watch (this technical man truly appreciates fine craftmanship and mechanics). And the one accessory to live for is a clean, tidy purse (in case he goes snooping through it). A bag full of crumbs and bills and trash could be fatal because, in his mind, a messy purse equals a messy (even dirty!) woman.

GIFT IDEAS: Those that are practical, technical, or useful

BEER BUDGET

Books (how-to, health, and medical reference)
Computer software or accessories
Box of herbal teas
Chess game
Workout clothes
Pen set

CHAMPAGNE BUDGET

High-tech daily organizer
Video camera
New computer
Encyclopedia set
Membership to a state-of-the-art health club
Expensive, reliable watch

ADD SOME SPICE

You might feel compelled to add some spice if life gets a bit bland. Just use discretion.

Some Ideas

1. Go over to his place wearing a sexy black dress, for no (apparent) reason.
2. Draw out some of his buried passion by making him insanely jealous.
3. Give him a (useful) present, just because you love him.
4. Send him an erotic film anonymously.

IF YOU SENSE A LOOMING BREAKUP

Mr. Virgo has better things to do with his time than spend it with the wrong girl. For that reason, he won't let a useless relationship drag on, unless he's unsure and still trying to determine the merits of it. Since he's not always fond of expressing his feelings, you'll have to pick up the clues to see where they lead and figure out what to do from then on.

Danger Signs to Watch For

- Increasing time at the office or gym
- A sudden interest in a hobby unrelated to you
- Emerging flakiness and last-minute behavior
- Even more criticism (of you or something related to you)
- Less sex

If you're feeling some rejection, take the matter into your hands. Inform him that his actions speak for him and the truth is out. He won't only realize how smart you are, he'll be relieved he didn't have to do any of the talking. Then go on to tell him that he's too perfect for you and could find someone better (yes, he'll pick up on the slight sarcasm in your voice). If he agrees, then you know it's time to split. But if he begins to whine or say he's not sure, there's still a chance (if you really want it).

In either case, let it be you who calls a time-out. Then let him get used to life alone again as you charge ahead with your own productive plans. You can bet he'll be analyzing the situation in the coming weeks, but don't return his calls unless he's had plenty of time to reassess the life he had with you. If you make another try at it, let him know it's you in charge from now on. (Then work on your weak points so you can enjoy a better relationship.)

AND NEVER FORGET

His essential need to be useful

HOW MR. VIRGO SEES YOU

	AT BEST	AT WORST
Aries	initiating, confident	daring, overly sexual
Taurus	reliable, earthy	self-indulgent, luxury-loving
Gemini	logical, interesting	capricious, irresponsible
Cancer	supportive, gentle	messy, illogical
Leo	strong, disciplined	extravagant, dramatic
Virgo	neat, intelligent	carping, inhibited
Libra	well-groomed, fair	expensive, frivolous
Scorpio	strong, devoted	excessive, exhausting
Sagittarius	interesting, optimistic	exaggerating, careless
Capricorn	economical, responsible	demanding, negative
Aquarius	clever, independent	unsettling, bizarre
Pisces	sympathetic, kind	disorganized, deluded

COUPLES COMPATIBILITY

BEST BETS	WHY NOT?	CHALLENGING
Taurus	Leo	Sagittarius
Capricorn	Libra	Pisces
Aries	Aquarius	
Scorpio	Gemini	
Cancer	Virgo	

VIRGO MAN (Hugh Grant) and GEMINI WOMAN (Liz Hurley)

These lovers can be great buddies—they both enjoy discussing the latest news and gossip, and just being informed of what's going on in the world around them. And they can take turns reassuring each other when they're feeling insecure. But the Gemini gal might eventually find Mr. Virgo a tad boring, and he might start seeing her as undisciplined and irresponsible. Still, the communication level (written or verbal) is usually strong, so these two will have a hard time letting go of each other. As for marriage, the prospects are nothing more than fair. The problem is that the Virgo man is always unsure and the Gemini woman always changes her mind. Besides, the Virgo man is naturally suspicious of marriage, and the Gemini woman can never be sure when she's made the *right choice* (and the more choices she has, the more fickle she gets). But it's okay. Even when they break up, they usually stay friends, since neither are the types of people tormented by savage passions and lustful revenge. No, this is a decent and pleasant pair that should always share company, if not as lovers, then as friends.

SOME ADVICE—TAKE IT OR LEAVE IT

YOUR SIGN	
Aries	DO: impress him with your ability to get things accomplished DON'T: demand sex when he's "not in the mood"
Taurus	DO: impress him with your financial savvy DON'T: indulge in too much food and drink
Gemini	DO: enjoy challenging conversations and lively debates DON'T: unnerve him by changing your mind all the time
Cancer	DO: offer him your loving support when he's down DON'T: get into his space and make a mess of it
Leo	DO: impress him with your self-confidence and pizzazz DON'T: ask him to take you shopping

Virgo	DO: help him plan a strategy to achieve his goals DON'T: get on each other's nerves
Libra	DO: flatter and charm him when he needs it DON'T: expect him to appreciate your busy social agenda
Scorpio	DO: impress him with the depth of your loyalty and support DON'T: turn him off with excessive moods, behavior, or habits
Sagittarius	DO: lift him up with your cheerfulness and good humor DON'T: overindulge in negligent behavior
Capricorn	DO: help him develop his long-term goals DON'T: make this harsh world seem even harsher than it is
Aquarius	DO: engage in brilliant conversations DON'T: unsettle him with your unpredictable behavior
Pisces	DO: let him know he can talk to you about anything DON'T: be completely illogical when you speak or argue

Looking Farther Down the Road

THE ENGAGEMENT

Engagement and marriage are touchy subjects with most Virgo men. You might wait a *long* time before he feels ready to take this step. Sure, he might be considering it, but it could take years until he fully analyzes the situation and decides that a life with you might be reasonable after all.

Sometimes he needs a little push. The danger is that if you're too eager or bossy, he could become suspicious, asking himself why you're in such a hurry to get hitched and what you might be trying to hide. And if your emotions get the better of you and you end up spewing it all out one night in a drunken fury, he'll be glad to discover that you're a hysterical mess after all, and won't hesitate to say good-bye. If you must broach the subject, always appeal to reason, not emotion, when discussing the merits of life à deux. You could even introduce the notion that marriage helps promote a "healthy," productive life.

THE WEDDING

The Virgo man will appreciate a woman who can sort through the long list of details involved in planning a wedding. So don't stress him out even more than he may be already by presenting him with different scenarios daily. Since Mr. Virgo likes perfect organization and hates unnecessary expenses, you might consider a package wedding—one reasonable price and no hassles (especially if he's footing the bill). Otherwise, think about a low-key wedding on a smaller scale.

Colleagues usually play an important role in this man's life, so be sure to include many of them on the invitation list. And don't invite friends who become crazy and obnoxious after a few glasses of champagne. You should aim for discretion and good taste, and it doesn't have to cost a lot. So forget frivolous and wasteful gimmicks and aim for moderation.

THE HONEYMOON

The best Virgo honeymoon is well-planned, minimizing the chance for hitches or unpleasant surprises. And it shouldn't be too wild, exhausting, or expensive. Many Virgo men love all-inclusive vacations, where they don't have to fret about extra or unnecessary costs. And let's not forget the health factor—food should be nutritious and fuel for the body, and it wouldn't hurt to have access to sports or a gym to burn off any (albeit unlikely) excesses.

Since most Virgo men detest sitting around doing nothing, forget the decadent vacation where the only activity is slurping down cocktails and lounging around. Bring some good books, find his favorite newspaper, and plan some interesting activities so your Virgo husband isn't dying to get back to work (one reason to keep the vacation short). Most important, don't overdo it yourself now that you're married. One night of disgusting excess or bewildering behavior may be enough to send him packing. Enjoy yourself in a wholesome way, stay productive, curb (hide) your bad habits, and your honeymoon should be a success.

Honeymoon Sex

Now that you're a legal couple, your Virgo hubby might feel more comfortable about sex than ever. This doesn't mean that he'll let out all his demons and surprise you in bed, but he should be more confident and strive to improve on past performance. Just make sure you're always clean and fresh—this Virgin will not feel amorous after a grimy and sweaty day of hiking. And if you want to venture to new sexual territories, be sure he is game.

MAKING IT IN THE LONG HAUL

The future should be smooth sailing once the Virgo man feels completely settled in his new life and habitat. But a lot of that depends on you and your ability to keep life orderly. Yes, he'll drive you absolutely mad with his nagging and complaining if you give him good reason. So just don't. And keep your marriage productive and rewarding as the years roll by. Make plans, help each other out, and keep the conversations interesting so he doesn't turn to his computer for mental stimulation. Above all, don't develop a destructive habit like drinking too much or binge eating that will threaten his respect for you.

DOS AND DON'TS FOR LASTING BLISS

DO

Keep your feet on the ground.
Make your house tip-top tidy.
Plan regular, healthy meals.
Keep well within your budget.
Stay attractive, mentally and physically.
Give him a boost when he turns pessimistic.
Let him nag when he really needs to.
Be up-to-date on current affairs.
Be interested in his work and colleagues.
Get him to talk about his problems when he closes up.
Brighten his days with a sunny demeanor.
Be perfect, organized, and clean.
Continue to work or pursue worthwhile pastimes.
Know how to save and recycle.
Keep interesting company.
Accept his helpful advice.

DON'T

Become a reckless spender.
Let yourself get lured into petty fights.
Fall apart when it's that time of the month.
Stress him out unnecessarily.

Overreact when he makes an observation you don't like.
Become an emotional mess.
Become addicted to destructive or disgusting habits.
Have grandiose fantasies and plans.
Sit around and do nothing.
Grow cold and stop giving him affection.
Make him feel he's not good enough (for anything).
Complain when he works overtime.
Party all night and sleep in till noon.
Begin neglecting your hygiene.
Make him insecure about your love.

EARTHLY BLISS (AKA SEX)

If you're a happy couple, your sex life should improve with time. Since the Virgo man tends to specialize, he might have a preferred technique or way of doing "it," striving each time to get it better. He might even make it a habit, and insist on certain days and times or even circumstances (like after a good body and teeth scrub). Eventually, you may want to open his eyes to more spontaneous and "exotic" lovemaking, as long as it's within the boundaries of good taste. You might even think about somehow getting a renowned and respected sex manual into his hands, since he's always interested in the technical aspect of things (though he might read it in secret). Sometimes a frigid Virgo man can warm up during a sexy movie, so make sure you have a supply of good DVDs, too. Just *never* make the mistake of criticizing his performance or making him feel ridiculous, especially when he's trying to impress you with something new. Only a very confident Virgo man can truly appreciate the many joys of sex, so make him feel like a winner in bed if you want the best of him.

Of course, there will be times when he's just not in the mood, or when he feels that his computer or new book has something more interesting to offer. And it's okay. The Virgo man doesn't need constant sex to stay happy. He can be just as content sitting in the TV room with his partner and reading the newspaper. Still, you don't want to regress to monthly sex, so find ways to get him in the mood. And if he's working overtime, make sure you schedule a lovers' evening (or lovers' lunch) into his busy agenda. Sex doesn't have to take too long, but it could be more frequent. Anyway, the Virgo respects maintenance, so he shouldn't mind regular servicing.

AND CHEATING . . . ?

You're pretty safe with a Virgo man, since sex and romance are not his reasons for living. And he just doesn't like his life to get messy, which is always a big risk when entering into illicit relationships. You just have to hope that he has no successful and attractive colleagues at the office, which is the one scenario that could be particularly threatening, especially if he's spending a lot of time there. And if it's in your power, try seeing to it that he doesn't hire a brainy and leggy secretary who can put his life in better order than you can.

Then there's always that computer to be leery of. Because the Virgin spends a lot of time online, it wouldn't be unfeasible for him to end up in an "e-mail relationship" with another woman, one that eventually leads to more. If he's spending too many hours at the keyboard, you might want to make sure his time there is spent on games or research instead of secret correspondence. And try encouraging him to take up interesting hobbies so he doesn't have time to think about other women. Still, in most cases you really have no reason to worry about your Virgo man, as long as you are nearly perfect and keep him satisfied.

REASONS HE MIGHT CHEAT

- If a perfect woman pursues him
- If you criticize him or his sex appeal
- If it conveniently works into his schedule

WHAT YOU CAN DO

- Make him feel like a great lover.
- Become close to his colleagues and drop by the office regularly.
- Criticize acquaintances you know who cheat (as in "How pathetic").
- Develop the sexual routine that fits perfectly into his life.

SOME THINGS TO TWEAK

As the years go by, you'll notice that your Virgo husband is never really satisfied. It could be something to do with work, finances, or health, or it could even be imaginary issues that give him a good excuse to complain. Or he'll take the most minor thing and make a huge deal about it. You have to get him to believe that nobody has a perfect life. Tell him that a perfect life is boring, anyway. Perfect people, too. And tell him how absolutely miserable he would be if his life were perfect. Sure, he'll ignore you or accuse you of insanity. But he'll also start thinking about your wise words in the days to come, slowly mulling them over in his head. And maybe, just maybe, you'll notice his next bout of criticism to be a bit milder than the previous ones.

Then you might try adding a little color and spontaneity to his orderly life. The Virgo man puts work way before fun, which is probably a good thing (at least for the rest of us). But still, if there's never time for amusement or excitement, life becomes a bit dreary. And so does his attitude. You might think of intelligent ways to coax him out of his routine, just to give him a needed break. And don't worry, the Virgo man is more adaptable than you think, so it shouldn't be impossible. Of course, he'll (fortunately) never agree to really foolish escapades or pointless adventures, so make sure you use some good sense when planning extracurricular activities. Time for play could do wonders for your Virgo lover—you just have to make him realize it.

AND HAPPILY EVER AFTER . . .

Life with the Virgo man should be healthy and productive. And it might even resemble a continuing-education class on self-improvement. If you can accept his critical advice over the years, he should help bring out the best in you, and what's wrong with that? So get real and forget the sexy lifestyle you might sometimes dream about—save yourself and let the other gals burn out at forty-five. You might not appreciate it now, but you'll be thankful when you make it to your golden anniversary (with enough energy to make it past midnight).

Libra, the Scales

(about September 23 till about October 22)

This man is a natural charmer, talented in the subtle art of seduction. A born diplomat, he tells girls things they want to hear. Sound sneaky? Not at all. This man simply likes people to feel good. So don't expect to get a completely honest answer all the time.

Like the Scales, the Libra man weighs everything out before making a decision, so his sense of justice can never be questioned. But this often results in hesitation and indecision and can annoy the hell out of a woman who expects a quick and firm decision. Still, he can't be rushed. His quest is to achieve a perfect balance in both love and life, and that can't be done under pressure. Anyway, his sunny smile and sense of fair play will surely win you over.

Highly aesthetic, the Libra man is especially weak for beautiful or artistic women, and he himself can be the one seduced by a woman if the time and moment are right. Does this mean he is unfaithful? Well, not really, at least not in his eyes. But even a Libra in love can occasionally fall into the trap of a very attractive woman. And yet it usually stays at the flirting level because his innate sense of justice prohibits it from going further. Even if he makes the occasional goof, it is not because he is not in love but, simply, in awe of beautiful women. This is the guy whose eyes will light up upon being introduced to a sublime female at a cocktail party, to the dismay of his girlfriend standing right next to him. But let him gawk from time to time. A beautiful woman is to be admired, just like a beautiful car or a beautiful painting.

The Libra man is no solitary creature. He hates to be alone, and it's a rare Libra man who doesn't have a girl by his side. Whereas other men need periods of being free and single, this one usually goes from one relationship to another, with no break in between. Think he's going to stay at home and cry when you leave him? Not a chance. The Libra man will have a new partner in minutes, so think twice before breaking it off.

Some women complain that the Libra man is superficial. Perhaps. At first you think you don't know him well enough and that in time you'll see his deeper side. Then you wait, and wait, and wait, and months (or years) later, you realize you still haven't reached any depths. What is this guy, a paper cutout? you ask yourself. Probably not. The Libra man might be as complex as the rest of us, but he's so busy perfecting the harmonious facade and enjoying cocktail parties that he doesn't have time to delve into deeper parts of himself. And then he forgets them himself, until the day arrives when something touches him to the core and he realizes there's something down there after all.

So, while you will probably never experience depths of passion and words of conviction with this man, chances are you'll maintain a good relationship that never risks exploding like dynamite. This is especially useful for the gal with a difficult personality, since the Libra man has the amazing capacity to absorb the egos of stronger, more selfish women. While other

THE LIBRA MAN IS

AT BEST	AT WORST
Charming	Superficial
Diplomatic	Hesitant
Aesthetic	Indecisive
Refined	Vain
Objective	Luxury-Loving
Attractive	Lazy
Intelligent	Weak-Willed
Sociable	Dependent
Cooperative	Easily Influenced
Popular	Contradictory
Cultivated	Snobbish
Fair	Compliant
Meditative	Shallow
Sophisticated	Insincere
Suave	Phony

men would throw you and your bags out the door in five seconds, the Libra man will usually ignore your "difficult" moments. He might turn to a good book or take a drive in his car until you gather your senses, but he won't tell you to go take a hike. And he certainly won't light the fuse—if anything, he'll try to calm you down with his soothing voice, because the Libra man craves harmony in relationships. Still, it's never wise to go overboard, because one dispute too many and the Scales could tip in another woman's favor. Just like that.

Eventually, Mr. Libra's harmonious facade can become annoying to the gal who wants to solve a critical problem in the relationship. He is a man who tends to sweep problems under the rug, as though not "seeing" them can make them nonexistent. But instead the problems hibernate there, waiting to haunt him at a future date. The Libra man just wants to wish all bad things away, and since he's more a man of today than tomorrow, he sells out for immediate harmony, not thinking that he'll pay big time later. You might be tempted to take off his rose-colored glasses and throw him into the blinding light of reality, but when you stop to think about it, you realize he's one of the happiest people around, so maybe there is some wisdom in viewing life through tinted lenses.

The good thing is that the Libra man has great respect for his partner, and will make no decisions without considering her side of things. Of course, he hopes she'll do the same. Sure, he'll be disappointed if she chooses to spend her free day with her best friend instead of him, because he hates to be left alone. But he'll keep his smile, as long as she seems happy (and as long as it doesn't happen too often). The Libra man feels completely balanced when he's in a beautiful relationship, so he'll do everything in his power to make sure there's harmony in the relationship, even if it means going against his own wishes. Isn't that sweet?

It's easy to understand what draws you to this fine and attractive man. And it might be a relief to finally hook up with one of the less difficult guys around. The months ahead should be smooth sailing with this guy as long as you are able to keep up a delightful facade. And if you really want to bedazzle him, share his hopes and dreams so he knows what real partnership is. You want to make life without you seem unthinkable.

SOME FAMOUS LIBRA MEN

Michael Douglas, Roger Moore, Matt Damon, F. Scott Fitzgerald, Vladimir Putin, John Lennon, Christopher Reeve, Tim Robbins, Mark Hamill, George Gershwin, Luciano Pavarotti, Ralph Lauren, Marcello Mastroianni, Truman Capote, Jimmy Carter, Gore Vidal, Gandhi, Charlton Heston, Jesse Jackson, Giuseppe Verdi, Dwight D. Eisenhower

MUST HAVE BEEN A LIBRA MAN

James Bond 007 (as interpreted by Roger Moore)

THE SEDUCTION

Get this man to notice you by appealing to his highly tuned aesthetic sense. No matter what he's doing or who he's with, his beauty radar can't miss a lovely, well-dressed female within a mile's radius. Still, even if he loses his breath, he usually won't show it. His eyes will sparkle and his friends will know what's going on, but he's too much of a gentleman to get hot and bothered over a woman.

The best bet is an introduction made by a third party, or a "random" collision somewhere, like in a bookstore or in the office cafeteria. Once your acquaintance is made legitimately, he'll feel more comfortable to begin his charm routine. And if he likes what he sees, he might even be so bold as to ask you out. But he'll always wait for the appropriate moment, and he has the patience to do so.

This is the man who appreciates the niceties of courtship. He could bring flowers, wine and dine you at expensive restaurants, and litter your path with little gifts. Let him play the prince if he wants, and know how to play the lady (dressed for the part). Dating and romance should stay fine and polished, and etiquette should never be taken lightly. And go ahead and flatter him from time to time—he can never tire of hearing how handsome and intelligent he is.

Once a connection has been established, the flirting and kissing can give way to more serious fare. But, like everything, the next step should occur at the suitable moment and in appropriate surroundings. When the moment is in full bloom, head for a beautifully draped bedroom and let this attractive man seduce you with finesse. And praise him for being a dream lover.

SEX

fine, romantic, complete

This cerebral man is not consumed with the purely physical aspect of sex, because it must appeal to his mind as well. Beauty and finesse go hand in hand in his approach to sex, so you don't want to shock him with vulgar or demeaning requests. To him, sex is more about making love and becoming "one." It should be romantic and inspiring and make him feel complete.

Seduction, both mental and physical, will always play a role in good sex. This is not the man you want to jump in the parking lot—you'll score more points with clever flirting and delicious eye contact. Even the dress you're wearing can put him in the mood for love. Just take your time and let his desire build—this is a man of patience, who knows that the best things never come too quickly. Same goes for sex—there's no reason to rush a good thing.

Because he's so accommodating, the Libra man might put your pleasure before his, just because it's so important to him to make his partner happy. (And you can't imagine how bad he'd feel to learn you didn't enjoy it!) This is one guy who will listen to your needs, so tell him what you want (unless it's something extreme, such as group sex or some S&M). But don't get selfish—there's no reason you both can't enjoy wonderful lovemaking.

DOS AND DON'TS OF A GREAT RELATIONSHIP

DO

Be well-groomed from head to toe.
Be feminine and classy.
Be sociable and fun.

Be a reasonably fair person.
Act as a team.
Consider him when making decisions.
Have attractive, respectable friends.
Enjoy parties and cultural activities.
Strive for harmony and peace in everyday life.
Make your surroundings beautiful.
Take the initiative when he hesitates.
Encourage him to assert himself when he wants something.
Be able to see different points of view.
Make sure to compliment his new clothes or haircut.
Allow him his occasional flirting (it's harmless).
Reassure him of your love (every day).

Be vulgar and rude.
Be unfit and sloppy (in private or public).
Have a screechy or whiny voice.
Be overly emotional or irrational.
Go looking for arguments and trouble.
Do things that embarrass him in public.
Pick fights with his friends and family.
Be in a bad mood all the time.
Let him see your messy bedroom.
Engage in illegal or shady activities.
Play cheap or low games with him.
Take advantage of his desire to please.
Put your girlfriends before him.
Be too independent and make him feel insignificant.
Leave him alone for too long.

BEST WAYS TO IMPRESS

Know how to sing an Italian opera aria (well).
Just be drop-dead gorgeous.
Be Ms. Society and the most gracious hostess.
Have a live-in beautician.
Flatter him (in public and private).

BEST WAYS TO GET DUMPED

Gain a hundred pounds.
Burp after a good meal.
Rip out his hair when you've had a bad day.
Make a horrific scene at a dinner party.
Adopt the "low-maintenance" look and stop shaving your legs.

FASHION

Naturally, the Libra man likes his women draped in beautiful clothes. To him, it's all about packaging and choosing the most attractive gift wrap for the box, so it's important that a woman have great taste (and an objective eye). Still, he may forgive a ravishing beauty if her fashion skills are not the best, and besides, he's the perfect man to consult when in doubt. He's even a great shopping partner because he's patient, aesthetic, and, most important, too much of a gentleman to let you pay!

Most Libra men appreciate the real woman, from breasts to willowy waists to tiny ankles. And the best clothes are those that accentuate the feminine assets while hiding the flaws. Still, not every look will do, like grunge or the hippie look. The Libra man loves clothes that convey class, femininity, and discreet sexiness (even glamour when the moment calls for it). And he has nothing against the most luxurious fabrics and best cuts.

Always the diplomat, he'll tell you that you look nice, but you'll know he really means it when his face alights in a fantastic smile.

Beyond the gift wrap, there are the ribbons and other decorative items to think about—precious jewelry, beautiful shoes, a stylish handbag. But probably most important is a perfectly groomed body—manicured finger- and toenails, silky, scented skin, white teeth, shiny hair, great breath, etc. No matter how beautiful the outfit, dirty fingernails or hairy armpits will not be pardoned.

GIFT IDEAS: Those that are fine, luxurious, or aesthetic

BEER BUDGET

Classical music CD
Picture frame
Fine chocolate
Cologne
Silk tie
Beautiful picture book

CHAMPAGNE BUDGET

Tickets to an opera premiere
Cashmere coat
Case of expensive champagne
Crystal vase
Designer anything
Beautiful painting

ADD SOME SPICE

Once the Libra man is settled into a relationship, he doesn't appreciate unpleasant occurrences. Still, some mild spice wouldn't hurt, as long as it's palatable.

Some Ideas

1. For once, get jealous when he flirts at a party and let him sleep alone that night.
2. Challenge him to *show* his feelings rather than talk about them.
3. Take a trip with your best friend so he sees what life is like without you.
4. Treat him to a tasteful private striptease.

IF YOU SENSE A LOOMING BREAKUP

The Libra man hesitates before making drastic decisions, especially those that can incite ugly words or teary scenes, so he rarely surprises a girlfriend with a rude and sudden "good-bye." Instead, he'll spend sleepless nights thinking about what to do, when to do it, and how to make a gracious exit when he's made up his mind (or met a replacement). And it's never easy to tell what he's really thinking or feeling, because he always tries to maintain his happy facade. An exceptionally perceptive girl, however, might be able to ferret out the truth.

Danger Signs to Watch For

- Increasingly superficial and meaningless conversation
- Less togetherness
- Decreasing sincerity in his smile
- Less tolerance for arguments and ultimatums

If you catch the truth before it's too late, you might still be able to smooth things out. This is the man you can talk to face-to-face, as long as you retain a loving, calm voice. He might even be relieved if you bring up the subject yourself and be happy to discuss the problem. Most obstacles are workable, and he's usually reasonable, so aim for some peaceful negotiations. Just never break out into an emotional fury and storm out of the room if he doesn't tell you what you want to hear.

If your Libra man is too nice to break bad news, but you're *sure* he's unhappy with you, back off and give him time to make up his mind. Let him get a sense of what life without you is like while you indulge yourself in some beauty treatments and new clothes. Wait until he sees you at the next party, when you're glowing and enjoying the attention of other attractive males. He might just try to charm you all over again.

AND NEVER FORGET

His essential need for beauty and harmony

HOW MR. LIBRA SEES YOU

	AT BEST	AT WORST
Aries	dynamic, decisive	aggressive, hasty
Taurus	sensual, serene	bossy, earthy
Gemini	sociable, intelligent	unassuring, nervous
Cancer	dependent, loving	moody, negligent
Leo	charismatic, luxury-loving	overbearing, inflexible
Virgo	adaptable, wholesome	anxious, critical
Libra	attractive, charming	hesitating, shallow
Scorpio	devoted, determined	intense, ruthless
Sagittarius	optimistic, fun	unsophisticated, tactless
Capricorn	status-seeking, cautious	serious, negative
Aquarius	interesting, friendly	independent, disinterested
Pisces	gentle, artistic	complex, unreasonable

COUPLES COMPATIBILITY

BEST BETS	WHY NOT?	CHALLENGING
Leo	Aquarius	Cancer
Libra	Taurus	Scorpio
Gemini	Aries	Capricorn
Sagittarius	Pisces	
Virgo		

LIBRA MAN (John Lennon) and AQUARIUS WOMAN (Yoko Ono)

These are two intellectual, breezy individuals, who place a high priority on friendship and companionship. One could guess that the Libra man will be more dependent on his partner than the sometimes detached Aquarius woman, and when a Libra man is really in love, he might even think he's found his soulmate. In any case, the Libra man in love wants to share everything with his partner—romance, business, hobbies, politics, etc. It's all about partnership. The Aquarius woman, on the other hand, is more focused on her own agenda. But she could prove to be clever, insightful, and helpful in all of her husband's endeavors. Whatever the future holds for this couple, it doesn't run a big risk of exploding, because both parties are so civilized. And if either of them is to face sudden change, it's the Aquarius woman who can handle it better. She's actually very good at change, and better equipped than the rest of us to acclimate to a new way of life.

SOME ADVICE—TAKE IT OR LEAVE IT

YOUR SIGN	
Aries	Do: focus your positive energy on making a great couple Don't: go looking for fights and conflict
Taurus	Do: indulge in your mutual love of the good life Don't: always insist on his seeing things from your point of view
Gemini	Do: delight him with your pleasant repartee Don't: run around with your buddies and leave him alone
Cancer	Do: pamper and indulge him Don't: be lazy about grooming yourself and your home
Leo	Do: display your fashion savvy and party know-how Don't: despise him for being weaker than you
Virgo	Do: show off your sense of neatness Don't: nag and make him feel unloved
Libra	Do: be the charming woman you can be Don't: let your relationship stay at the superficial level
Scorpio	Do: help him get in touch with his deeper layers Don't: erupt into dramatic displays of jealousy and cruelty
Sagittarius	Do: delight him with your optimistic outlook on life Don't: look too far yonder and make him feel insignificant
Capricorn	Do: exploit your talent for making the right friends Don't: be so pessimistic and harsh
Aquarius	Do: translate your original streak into tasteful glamour Don't: disappoint him with your need for freedom and change
Pisces	Do: play up your romantic and compassionate side Don't: wear him down with your excessive emotional needs

Looking Farther Down the Road

TRUE LOVE

THE ENGAGEMENT

The Libra man in love is happy in each stage of a relationship. So happy, that he might forget to take the next step. He figures it's fine now, everyone's happy, why take any risks that could come with a heavier commitment? He likes to wait things out, and is likely to weigh the pros and cons forever and ever until someone gently pushes him to make a decision. Or until he meets an even more lovely creature. That's what makes legalizing things so sticky—it takes away his options and leaves him no nice and easy escape route.

If you must give him a signal that it's time to get engaged, do it in a flirty way and charm the pants off him. Never attack him or make ultimatums. Your Libra lover needs to be deliciously seduced into taking the next step.

THE WEDDING

Once your Libra man has finally decided to tie the knot, he'll look forward to a beautiful and exclusive wedding party. But don't bother asking his advice—he'll only slow down the planning. Just keep him happy by letting him know you're in control and will produce the most tasteful wedding one could imagine.

Of course, that means a first-class affair—the best food and champagne, the most beautiful setting, decorations, and music. And no embarrassing speeches (you might want to tip off the best man before his traditional toast). This event should run smoothly, with no unwelcome surprises or unsavory characters dropping in. And don't drink too much—you wouldn't want to traumatize your new husband by stumbling on the dance floor in front of all his friends.

THE HONEYMOON

For the married Libra man, there's no better vacation than a romantic one with his lovely sweetheart. And he'll do anything to please her. Still, he'd be secretly miserable in a sketchy destination with questionable eating establishments, so don't insist on visiting an underdeveloped country or vacationing in a secondhand camper. Besides, he needs beautiful surroundings to be at his best, so indulge him if you really want to make him happy.

As long as he's comfortable and spoiled, your Libra hubby will be in no rush to return home. And as long as you continue to enchant him with your feminine charm and loving disposition, he will not look back to his bachelor days. Keep this trip especially pleasing and don't ruin it with even one ugly dispute. And make sure you have enough beautiful outfits to last throughout the trip.

Honeymoon Sex

Finding time for sweet love with your enamored Libra lover shouldn't be difficult. For him, that's what honeymoons are all about. Delight him with precious lingerie and nighties, dim the lights, and head for your sumptuous love nest when you're in the mood. Make the moment romantic, even a bit erotic, as you slowly seduce him like you never have before. Just make sure your skin is soft as silk and your breath is fresh as a baby's. It wouldn't hurt to have a bottle of champagne lying around, either.

MAKING IT IN THE LONG HAUL

The Libra man loves partnership, but not necessarily with the same partner over time. Still, he's reasonable and fair and should stay content in a marriage as long as it remains harmonious and pleasant. Issues that would erode other marriages are less problematic with the Libra man because he usually chooses not to acknowledge them. He could even put up with a selfish woman as long as she stays beautiful and keeps up the public facade. But he detests obscenity and hysterical scenes, probably because he can't ignore them. So, as long as your behavior is reasonable, the future should pose few problems.

DOS AND DON'TS FOR LASTING BLISS

DO

Maintain your regular beauty appointments.
Tell him you love him every day.
Plan romantic getaways.
Make your home as beautiful as it can be.
Entertain fine people regularly.
Get excited about his hopes and projects.
Try to see things from his point of view.
Express your thoughts when you are having problems.
Include him in all your plans (or at least give him the option).
Apologize sincerely when you have crossed the line.
Appeal to his sense of justice when you think he's being unfair.
Motivate him to achieve his goals.
Make everyday life pleasant.
Hide your flaws and work on your bad habits.
Enjoy discussing topics of interest.
Dress well around the clock.

DON'T

Go near him if you're experiencing bad PMS.
Point out the negative side of everything.
Provoke him or pick fights.
Mix with shady characters.
Engage in disgusting behavior.
Invite top models to your home.
Take advantage of his goodness.
Demand passionate and intense encounters.
Pick and pry at every little discrepancy.
Embarrass him at social gatherings.
Dye your hair black if he loves you blond.
Be grumpy and moody all the time.
Lose interest in him.
Become increasingly difficult as you age.
Walk around the house in baggy sweats and curlers.

EARTHLY BLISS (AKA SEX)

Sex will always be a very important part of lasting happiness because the Libra man views it as the true means of becoming "one." Even after a big argument, he needs lovemaking to ensure that things have been smoothed out. But let the prelude to sex stay romantic as the years go by—just because you've been together for ten years doesn't mean you should regress to rudimentary groping. Beautiful lingerie is a big turn-on with him, so you may want to invest in an entire arsenal of silky fabrications (and keep up the figure to wear it).

Sex is also a way of proving your love to him, so don't put it on the back burner as time goes by. It might even be of more importance in the future since the Libra man (secretly) fears losing his sex appeal and needs the reassurance that you still find him attractive. Even if your home begins to fill up with children, the right woman will always find time to seduce Mr. Libra. And you should be thrilled since this man is always out to please you.

AND CHEATING . . . ?

Again, your Libra man craves love and partnership, but not necessarily with the same female as the years roll by. One danger is being replaced by a "new and improved model" since this man is always bumping into young, beautiful women. Still, he wouldn't actively seek out another lover. Instead, he's usually the victim of another's seduction since he's too nice to say no. But it mostly stays within the bounds of harmless flirting—after weighing the pros and cons of extracurricular romance, the fair Libra man would feel horrible taking it further if he's in a good marriage.

On the other hand, if life with you becomes intolerable for one reason or another, the Libra man would feel justified, even obliged, to seek solace in the arms of another female. And if he falls in "love," he could even leave you for her. To make it a no-guilt decision, he'd happily reason that it's in your mutual best interests. Still, it would take a really bad marriage for him to call it quits, so don't give him a good excuse to do so.

REASONS HE MIGHT CHEAT

- If he is seduced by an unbelievably gorgeous woman (he's simply too weak to resist)
- If you let yourself get frumpy
- If you make everyday life a living hell

WHAT YOU CAN DO

- Stay beautiful.
- Make life with you pleasant.
- Make life without you seem impossible.
- Team up on plans, projects, even business (to strengthen your union).
- Reassure him of your love (regularly).
- Avoid hanging out with too-attractive women.
- Mention how sad it would be to grow old *alone*.

SOME THINGS TO TWEAK

Okay, so you finally figured out that your Libra man is preoccupied (obsessed?) with the appearance of things. Most people admire beautiful objects, but his aesthetic needs are unreasonable. And unhealthy, too. This is the man who can choose the least qualified person for the job, only because she has the best smile and the most beautiful legs. (This even goes for men, too.) Somehow he thinks good-looking people are "good" and unattractive people are "bad," and he *always* gives the good-looking ones the benefit of the doubt. In the long run, he can miss out on potentially great relationships just because he can't get past the look-factor. Point out that the pimple-faced neighbor he could have befriended might have been more likely to wake up at three in the morning and take him to the hospital than the good-looking stud who needed his beauty sleep. Accuse him of being a beauty snob and remind him of it each time he is eventually disillusioned or abused. After several bad experiences, he might finally start going deeper (and everyone will be happier).

Your Libra man also has the sweet, but unproductive, tendency to be a people-pleaser, accommodating everyone's wishes and desires even if they go against his own principles. The motive, again, is superficial—the Libra man wants present harmony and happiness, even if it means "giving in" rather than doing what's right. He simply can't tolerate tears and ugly scenes and ends up paying for it. People who get to know him start to take advantage of this weakness and end up manipulating him for their own selfish interests. The worst part is that in the long run, the problems become bigger ones, because your Libra man didn't want to acknowledge and take care of them before. Make him understand that he *must* stop being a pushover, for the sake of his marriage, if not himself. And make an impact by telling him that the victors are laughing behind his back and calling him a fool. He's extremely sensitive to how others see him and would rather grow old than feel like a chump.

AND HAPPILY EVER AFTER . . .

The future with your Libra man should be pleasant, at the very least. And a good marriage won't require herculean efforts on your part—just some regular beauty treatments, time on the StairMaster, and pretty clothes (okay, you can't be a total bitch, either). Sure, you'll get annoyed by his obsession with beauty, but at least he'll inspire you to look your best, and what's wrong with that? Just surround this man with a world of beauty and harmony and he'll bend over backward for you. And make him feel important, attractive, and *loved.* It doesn't get more complicated than that (and for some that might be reassuring).

Scorpio, the Scorpion

(about October 23 till about November 21)

Have you been hypnotized by a Scorpio man? Watch out, he's magnetic and powerful and, worst of all, he knows it! You can recognize a Scorpio man by his intense and probing eyes, which no mask can hide. But don't be fooled by his "casual" smile—he's just trying to put you off guard while he's figuring you out. This is the guy who will eventually uncover your weaknesses, so if the time ever comes for war, he knows just where to sting. Sounds dangerous? Could be, if you betray him.

On the flip side, the Scorpion can be wonderfully passionate and real. And he's usually looking for a relationship that has the power to transform him. Not one to fancy casual affairs, he's made for partnerships that are rich and profound. Still, not every woman can handle him, so it's best to think twice before entering the Scorpion Zone.

As you get to know him, you might notice a slight criminal element in the Scorpio man, usually manifested by his fascination with crime novels and psychological thrillers (and you should probably be aware that many famous killers and criminals have a strong Scorpio influence). Likewise, intrigues and scandals (both personal and political) fascinate this complex creature. In fact, the Scorpion is at his best in moments of crisis, which renew his energy and spur him into action. And you can be sure a relationship with him will see plenty of storms and crises, especially those fueled by jealousy and questions of power. Sometimes you'll wonder if this provocative creature is trying to rock the boat on purpose. And maybe he is, because he loves drama and difficult situations (whether he's aware of it or not). But he also loves coming out the winner (or at least the survivor) and will prove that he's a formidable rival.

The Scorpion's attraction to the "dark" is often manifested in his choice of woman. The Scorpion likes sexy females, even vamps sometimes, because he's seduced by their apparent "strength." Still, when it comes to a real relationship, this man often seeks a female who presents a "good" image to the world yet has the capacity to enslave him in the bedroom.

Sometimes a Scorpio man falls for a certain woman for no discernible reason. There's just *something* about her, something he can't decipher himself, but it's strong, undeniable, and intense. (And it's often exclusive to him, because others might ask, "What can he possibly see in her?") And because sex is so important to him, she has to elicit sparks, too. This man has no problem with a pretty face, but she must have that certain "something" as well that torments or fascinates him.

One of the most important issues for this man is trust. Can he trust you? Should he trust you? Does he trust you? Even after a woman passes his subtle tests, over and over again, and even after he convinces himself he can trust her, a tiny part of him never will, so he'll continue looking for clues or tips that could prove him right not to. That's why the best policy with him is honesty, especially if your behavior looks the slightest bit sketchy. In any case, this intuitive man will eventually figure you out, so it's better to be honest now than sorry later.

In a true relationship (not just a sexual one), the Scorpio man is sincere and profound. And if he's satisfied with the way things are evolving, he should stay true (but never easy!). In some of the more extreme cases, his love can become so intense that he can behave irrationally (he even has stalker potential). And if he feels his love is one-way, or if he feels betrayed, he can become vicious, destructive, or self-destructive. This is the man who often has those roller-coaster-type relationships. When it's good, it's fantastic. When it's bad, it's horrendous. But some women know how to bring out only the best traits of a Scorpio man, and those lucky women experience a relationship that's too amazing for words.

Any woman involved with this man must have the courage to deal with his jealousy and suspicion. Your Scorpio lover won't take flirting (or any other displays of infidelity) lightly, and he'll analyze your supposedly impure motives to death, drilling you until he solves the case. If he feels wronged, he could play out his anguish in dramatic, even violent, scenes. And he's an expert in manipulation and vindictive behavior. This might seem exciting for some women, but those with a more delicate psyche should strive to avoid situations that could bring out the Scorpio venom.

Unless a woman is exceptionally deceptive, she won't find it easy to lie to or hide secrets from him. The Scorpio man can usually smell intrigue, probably because he's so good at it himself, and he'll deprive himself of sleep until he unravels a mystery. This is also a man who loves to snoop and eavesdrop, so it'd be wise to burn incriminating papers and photos. When he's dying to know something, he can even break codes and decipher passwords, so it's never a good idea to feel safe if there's something to hide. Sometimes a woman might even wonder if her Scorpio lover has X-ray vision.

The Scorpion is one of the most fascinating and complex men of the zodiac. If you can inspire him to display his positive (and not negative) traits, you will have one of the most devoted and worthwhile men out there. In any case, a relationship with this man, whether it lasts or not, will be unforgettable, and your memories of him could elicit extreme feelings—love *or* hate. So if you've been locked in a boring and passionless relationship, it may be time to date a Scorpion. But a warning to all hopefuls out there: Don't play games with this man unless you want to get stung!

THE SCORPIO MAN IS

AT BEST	AT WORST
Intense	Extreme
Magnetic	Jealous
Profound	Possessive
Exciting	Vindictive
Daring	Unyielding
Courageous	Rebellious
Surviving	Power-Hungry
Loyal	Hurtful
Intuitive	Secretive
Sexy	Prying
Regenerating	Self-Destructive
Mysterious	Provocative
Shrewd	Violent
Intriguing	Exhausting
Emotional	Obsessive

SOME FAMOUS SCORPIO MEN

Leonardo DiCaprio, Larry King, Ted Turner, Bill Gates, Larry Flynt, Martin Scorsese, John Gotti, Matthew McConaughey, Carl Sagan, Charles Bronson, Charles Manson, Pablo Picasso, Theodore Roosevelt, Fyodor Dostoyevsky, Richard Burton, "Lucky" Luciano, Robert Louis Stevenson, Prince Charles, Calvin Klein, Sean Combs, Dr. Martin Luther King Jr.

MUST HAVE BEEN A SCORPIO MAN

Rick Blaine *(Casablanca)*

THE SEDUCTION

To attract this man's interest, you'll have to maintain an air of mystery that inspires the natural detective in him. This is not the man to be impressed by a loudmouth who recounts her life story in five seconds, or the clown who's always cracking jokes. The best approach is discreet sex appeal and some smoldering stares, the kind that give him tingles in both his head and groin.

If you've managed to capture his attention, he'll be watching you in the days to come. And if you've really made an impact, he could even begin following you! Okay, not all Scorpions go this far, but even the more benign ones have a slightly predatory nature. In any case, what he learns in the following days will either intrigue him more or cool him off.

If he finally asks you out, maintain the image that attracted him so much in the first place. And don't volunteer any information. He doesn't need to know you have a yoga class on Thursday night—tell him you're busy but don't offer more. And when you do begin dating, keep him guessing. But that doesn't mean acting nonchalant or flighty—he'll want to know you find him attractive, so do so without giving yourself entirely away. Just know that after a few dates you're "his," because he won't accept being just one of your admirers.

It's never a good idea to surrender too easily to this man. He enjoys a challenge and overcoming obstacles. But when you know the moment is right, give in to his passion and let yours run freely. If the alchemy is there, you'll both know it after the first sexual encounter. But if the first time is a total washout, consider your relationship null and void.

SEX

intense, passionate, consuming, dangerous

"Sexual prowess appreciated—no virgins, please." This could be the Scorpio man's motto in the sex department. Of course, all of us are virgins at one point in our lives but, even then, some girls display more natural potential than others. And years of experience later, some are just better at sex and enjoy it more. The Scorpio man takes sex very seriously, so a female who is unskilled in bed or "barely there" won't last with him.

At the most basic level, sex is a necessary form of "release" for his pent-up energy, and it's better that he vents it in bed than through a dangerous sport or violence. Still, the most rewarding sex is more than just a physical act to him. It's a complex issue, one that should be emotional, spiritual, and transformational. It's also a manifestation of power. (Power, control, sex, and money are important themes in this man's life, though he may never admit it.) But that never means it has to be easy and merely pleasant. If anything, the real Scorpio man gets a (perverse) thrill out of sex tinged with excitement, risk, or even danger. But he won't necessarily let you in on that secret. Fortunately, intensity and passion (and a tiny bit of suffering) should be enough to keep him satisfied. Along with a woman who is strong enough to challenge him in bed.

Still, there's never a time to get smug. Just when you think you've found the key to this mysterious act, you'll learn that you have a long way to go. Ideally (but not practically), each sexual experience should reach new depths of pleasure (even pain!), with the potential for self-transformation. Sounds exhausting! And it is for most females. It's hard enough just knowing what's right and how far to go, let alone the rest of it. The best guide in uncharted territories is your own intuition. And whatever the ultimate outcome, the sexual journey should be an interesting one. (And that's putting things lightly.)

DOS AND DON'TS OF A GREAT RELATIONSHIP

DO

Be slightly provocative.
Be complex and intriguing.
Be able to hold his unwavering gaze.
Give him reason to trust you.
Cultivate your sex appeal.
Keep some secrets about yourself.
Display character and strength.
Be able to take on a dare.
Know when he's "testing you" (and be able to pass).
Stay calm and collected when he vents.
Allow him his privacy.
Take his secrets to the grave.
Encourage him in his quest for power.
Support him completely during his low periods.
Be passionate about *something.*

DON'T

Be frigid and cold.
Be superficial and silly.
Be too direct and frank.
Be untouchable, emotionally or physically.
Pry into his private affairs.
Volunteer to talk about ex-boyfriends.
Be friendly with any of his enemies.
Deny him of sex or use it for power (that's *his* department).
Trivialize his emotions.
Mock his intensity.
Give him reason to doubt you.
Screw with his mind (unless you're an expert in that field).
Have a casual or nonchalant attitude about your relationship.
Let him feel he's being "used."
Ever betray him.

BEST WAYS TO IMPRESS

Give him the orgasm of his life.
Be as sexy and dangerous as a Bond girl.
Work for the CIA and have juicy inside info.
Know your G-spot.
Be part of the power set.

BEST WAYS TO GET DUMPED

Become a born-again virgin.
Tell him you don't know how to have an orgasm.
Sleep with his archenemy.
Have absolutely no vices.
Get caught in a gross betrayal.

FASHION

The Scorpio man enjoys fashion because it has the power to convey a message, and the best message a female could send to a man is that she's confident, sexy, and exciting. Still, it doesn't have to be too obvious—a suggestion is more fascinating than a fact. But to really make it work, the attitude has to match the clothes. (And don't worry, he won't be upset if you can afford very expensive threads.)

A winning look is an outfit with just one "sexy" feature (e.g., a long slit, nude back, bare shoulders, some cleavage). Showing too much is never sexy because it leaves no room for imagination. Some Scorpio men even get turned on by a conservative outfit, one that keeps him guessing what good things lie beneath. Fortunately, you can never wear too much black with him, so dressing doesn't have to be that difficult. A Valentino red can turn him on, too.

Like the clothes, accessories say a lot. You can never go wrong with a great pair of dark sunglasses. They don't just say "attitude," they say "mystery" and "cool." Sexy shoes and high boots might also intrigue. Just stay away from super-trendy items that every girl has—the only message they send is "unoriginality." If in doubt, just reach for your best perfume and sprinkle your erogenous zones.

GIFT IDEAS: Those that pertain to his love of mystery, power, or deep emotions

BEER BUDGET

Dark sunglasses
Great mystery novel
Sexy cologne
Silk boxers
Classical music CD
Self-written poem

CHAMPAGNE BUDGET

Fine pajamas
Expensive red wine
Power briefcase
Pair of walkie-talkies
High-power telescope
Black sports car

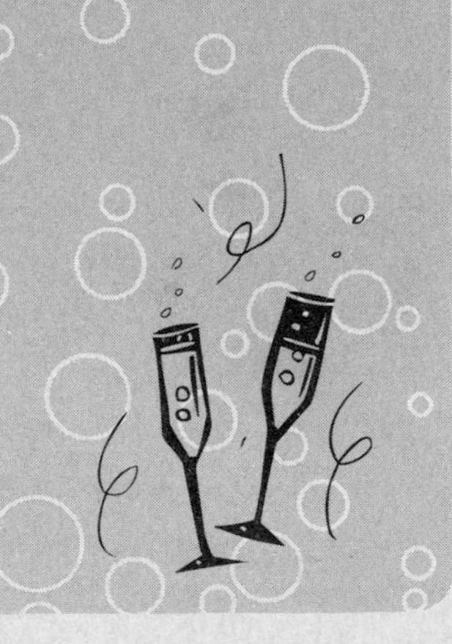

ADD SOME SPICE

Things will probably be spicy enough with this man. But go ahead and make things really hot if you want to.

Some Ideas

1. Become so passionate about a hobby or cause that he fears he'll lose you.
2. Flirt with danger, then take the adrenaline back to the bedroom.
3. Blindfold him, tie him up, and take total control of the situation.
4. Get into an explosive fight, then make up with electrifying sex.

IF YOU SENSE A LOOMING BREAKUP

When a Scorpio man is unfulfilled in a relationship, it's just a matter of time before he kills it off. During the breakup, he doesn't even mind tearful scenes (unless he's in *love*), because they add some excitement and drama to the day. Still, a break could come out of nowhere, with no warning. But a very intuitive female should be able to sense trouble ahead of time.

Danger Signs to Watch For

- Increasingly covert actions
- Increasing coldness
- More difficult behavior
- Less respect for you

If the problem is sexual incompatibility, there's not much you can do, unless you take a crash course in the Joys of Sex and become an expert overnight. But if you think your Scorpio boyfriend is simply growing weary of *you,* probably because he knows you inside out and there's nothing left to discover, try surprising him with some unprecedented behavior, the kind that will make him wonder if he ever really knew you in the first place. You can't imagine how unsettled (even intrigued) he'd be to realize he "misjudged" you and was, in fact, dealing with a stranger.

This is also the time to let your rebel side shine—your Scorpion would be shocked (and fascinated) to discover his little rose has some sharp thorns after all. And if you're great at psychological games, this may be the moment to use them (but tread with caution). No matter how you choose to go about it, aim for sparking his curiosity—he should be losing sleep trying to figure you out.

If, no matter what, the Scorpio man announces D day, you'd better just accept it. And try to get out of his life as soon (and as neatly) as possible. Resorting to vindictive behavior is dangerous with this one, so just pack your bags and go. Even if you plotted a vindictive act, like letting air out of his tires, would it really make you feel better? The only thing it would do is invite a mega-revenge, so gather your senses and disappear.

And don't worry about your Scorpio man. Crises and change are themes in his life—he'll do just fine, and might even be stronger the next time around. It isn't impossible for a Scorpion to reunite with an ex-girlfriend at a future date, but chances are that when he said good-bye, he meant it. And if you bump into him at a party in the future, don't let him lure you drunkenly back to his pad for some intense, nostalgic sex—he's probably just curious to see if he still has power over you.

AND NEVER FORGET

His essential need to survive

HOW MR. SCORPIO SEES YOU

	AT BEST	AT WORST
Aries	passionate, dynamic	direct, belligerent
Taurus	physical, loyal	inflexible, greedy
Gemini	complicated, clever	nosy, insincere
Cancer	nurturing, emotional	inconstant, conservative
Leo	loyal, great in bed	bossy, overpowering
Virgo	reliable, self-sufficient	modest, dispassionate
Libra	supple, unselfish	shallow, frivolous
Scorpio	intense, magnetic	jealous, vindictive
Sagittarius	adventurous, tolerant	carefree, simple
Capricorn	ambitious, faithful	frigid, harsh
Aquarius	interesting, unusual	aloof, untouchable
Pisces	compassionate, enigmatic	weak-willed, betraying

COUPLES COMPATIBILITY

BEST BETS	WHY NOT?	CHALLENGING
Cancer	Capricorn	Gemini
Pisces	Leo	Aquarius
Taurus	Scorpio	
Virgo	Sagittarius	
Aries		

SCORPIO MAN (Richard Burton) and PISCES WOMAN (Elizabeth Taylor)

This pairing is the kind you see in the movies, the kind you believe too intriguing for real life. But when a Scorpio man and Pisces woman come together, they have the potential to carry out the type of relationship that the rest of us only dream about. That doesn't mean it's picture perfect all the time—in fact, these two creatures have a tendency toward volatile and tempestuous romances. But the passion is there, one that most other people on earth aren't even aware of, which may be a good thing, because it's also the kind of passion that can only burn out. The Scorpio man is sometimes too intense and raw for the Pisces woman, who lives in an idealistic fantasy world where everything is romantic and fantastic. And when affairs of the heart go wrong, both signs have a tendency for self-destructive behavior. The funny thing about a Pisces woman is that it's not always over when it's over—she can flee a lover, only to swim back and enjoy more torrid (and fleeting) moments with him. And this scenario works out well for Mr. Scorpio, reassuring him that his sexual power is difficult to escape. Really, stuff made for the movies!

SOME ADVICE—TAKE IT OR LEAVE IT

YOUR SIGN	
Aries	DO: attempt to be more complex and mysterious DON'T: attack him with your direct line of fire
Taurus	DO: transcend your materialism to discover the deeper meaning of life DON'T: be unmovable just to prove your strength
Gemini	DO: work on reaching your deeper emotional levels DON'T: talk all the time
Cancer	DO: support him emotionally as he goes after his goals DON'T: let him mistake your capriciousness for infidelity
Leo	DO: enjoy charged, passionate sex DON'T: challenge him in the arenas of power and control
Virgo	DO: impress him with your self-control and discipline DON'T: criticize his sexual urges and other excesses

Libra	DO: let him know how complete he makes you feel DON'T: bore him with your phony or vacuous antics
Scorpio	DO: enjoy discovering every facet of each other DON'T: let jealousy, power plays, and suspicion destroy your relationship
Sagittarius	DO: curb your tomboy side and cultivate more sex appeal DON'T: take him lightly
Capricorn	DO: be a precious aid to helping him realize his dreams DON'T: be cold or inhibited in the bedroom
Aquarius	DO: intrigue him with your unique personality DON'T: chill him out with your nonchalant, detached air
Pisces	DO: tantalize him with your enigmatic allure DON'T: just give up and swim away when problems arise

Looking Farther Down the Road

TRUE LOVE

THE ENGAGEMENT

A Scorpio man who loves you intensely will want to make you all his, as soon as he is convinced that he can really trust you and that you are for real. If he fell hard from the very beginning, he might even scare you a bit with his desire to possess you permanently. But if things got off to a shaky start, it may take many tests and crises to overcome before he realizes that he wants you (or doesn't) for his wife. As long as your relationship continues to evolve positively, a proposal might come.

On the other hand, if your Scorpio man remains closed and secretive and never even refers to the future, he may not be ready for the next step. Instead of losing time, you might want to test him a bit, but in a way that is nonthreatening. Maybe you could mention that your love for him is so intense that you can't function anymore and that you are thinking about seeking a more bearable relationship. Or maybe you could beg him to be *kind* and let you go. Appeal to drama, intensity, and emotions, not logic and reason. If he sets you free, be happy that you learned the truth now rather than later. Rest assured, though, a Scorpio man will not say good-bye if he really loves you.

THE WEDDING

The prying Scorpio man will want to know what kind of plans you're making, but keep him a bit in the dark. Of course, if he insists on knowing a few details or has a special request, give in. But try to do a lot of behind-the-scenes planning to keep him intrigued.

Most Scorpio men prefer intimate and meaningful celebrations to light and fun ones, so avoid a wedding party that even remotely resembles a circus. Don't invite everyone in the world. This is a private affair, worthy of real friends. Most of all, don't make the mistake of inviting men you've slept with (or wanted to)—your jealous Scorpio lover could leave you stranded at the altar, at best.

THE HONEYMOON

It's possible that this man will do his own covert planning for the honeymoon, and if he stays true to his character, he'll probably choose a "sexy" destination. Wherever you end up, make the most out of every single moment. But save your best face for nighttime, when the Scorpion is in his "element." And don't worry about risque behavior or excesses—this trip should be as exciting as it is intense.

Most of all, your honeymoon should be a profound experience, one that surpasses all previous trips and events. Any casual or cool post-wedding behavior on your part could make him seethe in anger. Don't read a book if he wants to go exploring—you wouldn't want to appear aloof. To get the best out of your Scorpio husband, let him feel your emotional high. And be sure to make him feel sexy.

Honeymoon Sex

Your first married sexual experience should be utterly orgasmic! It would be wise to hold off on sex for one month before the honeymoon so the yearning is even greater. (But be sure your Scorpio man knows why you're doing this, so he doesn't suspect that someone else is satisfying you.) When the time comes, don't put on a coy charade or resort to technically correct seduction plans. Let it happen at night, maybe after a close encounter with danger when his emotions are still reeling. Mystify him, intrigue him, let him suffer a bit (or let him inflict a bit of suffering on you). Then, just when he thinks he has you completely in his grip, surprise him by cooling off until the tables turn and it is *he* begging for more. Make the experience *intense.*

MAKING IT IN THE LONG HAUL

This is the time to show your Scorpio man the depth of your commitment—he'll want to know you're behind him one hundred percent. If you take things too lightly or nonchalantly now, he might think you underestimate the power of wedding vows, and any other casual behavior could bring out destructive tendencies in him. Now that you've made it this far, don't think the future will become easier with time. A long-term relationship with a Scorpio man can be emotionally exhausting and intolerable for women with fragile mental or emotional health. If married life is running along smoothly, your Scorpio man might create problems just to add more friction to daily life. In the years to come, there will be highs, lows, and lots of waves that will test the strength of your marriage. Indulge him in his need for crises when you must, but know how to stand your ground and never become a pitiful victim. You'll be *relieved* when a huge political scandal breaks out on the world scene so he can channel his dark energy into following up on the latest developments and intrigues. (Take advantage of this time to regain your inner tranquillity.)

DOS AND DON'TS FOR LASTING BLISS

DO

Maintain a certain mystique.
Put up with his dark moods.
Take his side when he's been wronged (even if it's a bit his fault).
Help him regenerate when he's hit an all-time low.
Stand by your principles.
Cultivate at least one hobby.
Strive for success at work.
Encourage him to channel his inner energy through an intense sport.
Know how to make friends with people who could help him.
Stay sexy and attractive.
Maintain your bond with several other intimate and interesting couples.
Plan secret nighttime rendezvous.
Seduce him when he's least expecting it.
Know how to calm him down when he's on edge.
Let him know that he can always count on you.

DON'T

Resort to viciousness or revenge when angry (you're above that).
Meet ex-lovers for lunch.
Hang around when he's in a destructive mood.
Be too easy and give in just to avoid a scene.
Stab him in the back *(ever!)*.
Try to force his secrets out.
Cool off toward him.
Put your girlfriends and social life before him.
Waste your time on silly activities.
Lose interest in sex.
Let the mental and emotional games go too far.
Become lazy and inactive.
Tell him all your secrets.
Take him for granted.
Stay in a relationship that becomes totally destructive.

EARTHLY BLISS (AKA SEX)

Sex with your Scorpio man will never be dull! At least it shouldn't be if you want to survive the next few decades with him. Your sex life should reach new dimensions in the years to come, and not just physical dimensions, but emotional and spiritual ones as well. Here's a man who loves to go to extremes, so don't be shocked if he pulls out some handcuffs sometime in the future. No, he's not a sex maniac, but he'd love to explore the darker venues of sexual experience if he can be sure he can trust you.

Even after years together, sex will never be a simple affair. He wants to feel so many things at once—power, rapture, depth, pain, ecstasy, love, obsession . . . blurring together into one intense experience. At least this is what he thinks sex should be. Lucky for him if you are a willing partner. And lucky for the both of you if you can take turns astounding each other.

Of course, a fulfilling sex life is crucial to long-term happiness. If things cool off in the bedroom as time goes on, he could torture himself with the idea that your relationship is dying, or already dead, and then all the darker sides of his character could slowly surface, or he could have some sort of crisis. To avoid this, keep up your sexual energy and interest as you age, no matter what it takes. And think up new ways to keep sex exciting.

AND CHEATING . . . ?

Contrary to what you may have thought, the Scorpio man is not some sex fiend who lives for endless sexual encounters. When he's in a great marriage, and when he can experience sexual nirvana with his wife, he can stay very loyal and true.

But if things aren't going well, he does have the potential for some devious behavior. One scenario is "revenge" sex. If you betray him physically or emotionally, he might seek out another woman just to punish you.

Then there's the "top-secret" sexual affair. If your Scorpio man meets a woman who absolutely bewitches him, he could get involved in a risky and illicit liaison. The turn-on can be an extension of living "dangerously" or the thrill of cover-ups and "classified" affairs. Whatever the case, you would probably never know, anyway, since the Scorpio man is an expert at covering his tracks.

Still, the Scorpio man is not looking for a quick fling, but a woman who can help him evolve and transform. If that sexy and deep woman is you, he shouldn't deceive you.

REASONS HE MIGHT CHEAT

- If you cannot fulfill his sexual needs
- If you betray him
- If you become dispassionate and aloof
- If he meets a woman he *must* have
- If he needs to add some drama to a boring marriage

WHAT YOU CAN DO

- Add some spice to your life together.
- Know how to sexually captivate him.
- Continue to intrigue him with a little mystique.
- Tell him a loyal man is much stronger and sexier than a weak adulterer.
- Tell him you'd leave him forever if he cheats.

SOME THINGS TO TWEAK

The Scorpio man (and those around him) would enjoy life more if he could put a handle on his darker vibes and jealous nature. No, you can't change him, but you could encourage him to take up an old hobby, something creative or athletic, to provide an outlet for his inner turmoil. Kickboxing or surfing are two of the more exciting pursuits that could burn his dark energy. And if he is consumed by jealousy or vengeance, help rid him of his demons by pushing him to write a dramatic novel and getting it "all out" of his system. Maybe even a diary would work. One of the biggest obstacles to his happiness is pent-up frustrations, fears, and obsessions, so help him find a "healthy" way he can vent before he destroys everything worth living for.

It would also help if this man could learn to trust others more readily. It's not like the whole world is out to get him, and most people out there are actually pretty decent. He could have more rewarding friendships and more worldly success if he would stop being so suspicious of others' motives, and so unforgiving and vindictive when he feels he's been wronged. Encourage him to open up more, even if it makes him vulnerable. In the unlikely case of betrayal, he can take it as a learning experience rather than a stab in the back. Anything in life can be taken positively or negatively. Let him know that he alone has the *power* (he likes this word) to make himself happy. Or miserable.

AND HAPPILY EVER AFTER . . .

Life with Mr. Scorpio will never be a bore. Just when you think you've been through it all, a new crisis or development can emerge that will test your marriage . . . again. The only constant throughout the years will be transformation (for better or worse), and if you're strong enough to handle it, this relationship could be intensely rewarding and long-lasting. So make a decision to cherish your engrossing marriage and pity those women imprisoned in dull conjugal life. Not every wife of a Scorpio man can shout "I survived!" after fifty years of marriage, but those who do will be stronger than the rest of us.

Sagittarius, the Archer

(about November 22 till about December 21)

Attention, girls! This fun-loving juvenile is one of the hardest guys to capture, for more than a few days, at least. The nomad of the zodiac, this Archer aims his arrow toward far-off places and new horizons offering adventure and the element of the unknown. This is the guy who's been the best man at dozens of weddings, but never the groom. Marriage is just such a limitation (not to mention boring), though he'd be up for a honeymoon to an exotic island any day.

It's easy to understand how you fell for a Sagittarius guy, because there's something so lovable about him. He's the eternal child, always excited about something, always on the move, always bringing happiness to those around him. He loves the good life, and that certainly includes women. Just don't take his flirting too seriously. You might be the focus of his attention for one night, but could be easily replaced at the next party when a more exotic creature enters the room.

The Archer has undoubtedly left a trail of broken hearts behind him, but not because he is cruel. He just doesn't understand that the girls he plays with actually fall in love with him. He wouldn't hurt you on purpose, because he has a big heart and a sense of fair play. But his need for freedom and adventure can dominate him, making him unable to commit to even the loveliest of creatures.

However, if you are really set on getting this guy, there are ways you can date him while making him still believe he's free. Encourage him to go out with the boys, or take off to Vegas, or not call you for a few days (or weeks). If you really made any sort of impact on him in the first place, he should be back to charm you all over again, and each exchange may take things to a deeper level. Also, be ready for adventure yourself, and try planning a fun trip to a far-off place together (okay, since most of us work, you might have to settle for a weekend getaway). If the trip goes well, he might realize that it's more fun traveling in a pair. In any case, show him that a relationship with you does not mean a loss of his freedom.

The Sag man likes all kinds of women, but a well-rounded gal has the best chance of keeping his interest. A girl who is smart yet spirited might have more in common with him than the serious career girl who lives at the office six days a week. His partner needs lots of time for adventure and leisure, so those gals who are self-employed or work freelance are probably better suited to the Archer's rhythm. He also tends to like party girls, but they have to be clever and witty instead of blasé and burned-out. And there's something about foreign women that simply fascinates him.

The Sagittarius man has a direct approach with people, to the point of being blunt sometimes. No, this guy doesn't mean to be a jerk when he confirms that your butt is, indeed, big—he just feels he owes it to you to be honest. Anyway, it's better to know you have a big rear end than to wear the wrong pants, right? And if your relationship ever grows deeper, you can depend on him for honest advice on career moves, family matters, and friendships. This guy is like your brother and he'll treat you like the sister he never had (or the one he doesn't see too much of nowadays). Even if you can't count on a romantic commitment, you can count on a friend.

Another thing you can't always count on are his promises. He means them when he makes them, but when the time comes to deliver, he is usually off on another pursuit, and if you confront him, he might not even know what you are talking about. In time, you'll also notice that the Sagittarius man can get so swept away with his stories that he stretches them farther and farther each time he recounts them. Don't worry, it's not inspired by any impure motives. The Sag man just likes to tell a good tale and keep people entertained. And he also likes you to know all the cool people he knows and places he's been, though you'd better take it with a grain of salt when he tells you he's buddies with Madonna.

For the more evolved Sag man, there's often a great love for mind-opening subjects, like philosophy, religion, space, the meaning of life, etc. In case you're completely clueless about some of his more cherished topics, at least try to be open to them, no matter how esoteric they might seem to you. This Sag would be pleasantly surprised to meet a girl who understands where he's coming from.

THE SAGITTARIUS MAN IS

AT BEST	AT WORST
Adventurous	Risk-Taking
Optimistic	Naive
Carefree	Irresponsible
Lucky	Idealistic
Enthusiastic	Exaggerating
Fair	Blunt
Evolved	Sloppy
Philosophical	Impractical
Spiritual	Careless
Direct	Rude
Freedom-Loving	Nomadic
Fun	Hedonistic
Adaptable	Unreliable
Athletic	Restless
Knowledgeable	Lofty

The Sagittarius man has lots of fun things in store for you. Just don't push for a commitment, and *never* push marriage. If you become a great friend and listener and the two of you have sexual chemistry, this Archer might finally realize that you could make his life that much richer. In any case, he should brighten your life and put a smile on your face.

SOME FAMOUS SAGITTARIUS MEN

Steven Spielberg, Brad Pitt, John Malkovich, John F. Kennedy Jr., Ed Harris, Kenneth Branagh, Scott Joplin, Andrew Carnegie, Charles Schulz, Jimi Hendrix, Bruce Lee, Mark Twain, Richard Pryor, Woody Allen, José Carreras, Jim Morrison, Kirk Douglas, Frank Sinatra, J. Paul Getty, Ludwig van Beethoven, Billy the Kid, Walt Disney

MUST HAVE BEEN A SAGITTARIUS MAN

Indiana Jones *(Raiders of the Lost Ark)*

THE SEDUCTION

It won't be long before the Sag man's roaming eye spots you. The best scenario would be if this took place in some exotic spot abroad, but since that might be impossible, an everyday situation could work well, too. There're so many things that could draw him to you, and if he likes what he sees, he won't be bashful in approaching you. This is the guy who likes to take risks, so he won't hold back out of fear of rejection. And he's so confident of his charms that he wouldn't even consider a rejection possible, anyway.

It might not be a bad idea to make him question his charm, so don't give in right away when he asks you out. And never cancel your plans to accommodate his schedule. Yes, you might find him absolutely irresistible, but you don't have to show it!

And besides, the Sag man likes a good challenge, so never make things too easy for him.

When you do start dating, play around with him from the beginning, and let him guess a lot. Things don't have to get hot and heavy from the start—a lighter approach might work better. Keep the "relationship" light and fun and *never* make a scene if he flirts with another girl at a party. He doesn't "belong" to you, at least not yet.

When you really start to feel comfortable with him, let the playful kisses and flirting give way to more serious fare, even if it's sooner rather than later. (This is not the guy to judge your behavior if it's fueled by true enthusiasm and joy.) Just don't get all heavy on him once you've slept together. Stay casual yet enticing so he doesn't feel restricted.

SEX

fun, lively, enthusiastic, casual

The Sag man is always up for a good tumble in the bed (or anywhere else). And why not? It's fun and positive. And it feels great, too. But he sees sex as a casual matter, so it doesn't have to *mean* anything but a good time. And it could be that much better if you don't "expect" anything, either.

No, this is not the guy to get all soppy with emotions during sex. And demanding mushy romantic foreplay or afterplay might only turn him off. Sure, he's full of zest and enthusiasm, but not for bearing his heart and soul. So those gals expecting some profound emotional response in bed might be disappointed. But it's nothing against you—he's just like that, with you and all the other gals, so save the tears for someone else and just enjoy the moment.

The Sagittarius man has a low boredom threshold, so Monday Night Only Missionary Sex might send him off in search of more stimulating company. This guy is always on the lookout for new and interesting ways to fool around, so tickle him pink by staying open-minded and willing. Still, it wouldn't hurt to take some wind out of his sails from time to time so he doesn't go around thinking he's God's gift to humanity. You can't imagine how quickly his you-know-what can go to his head.

DOS AND DON'TS OF A GREAT RELATIONSHIP

DO

Be challenging and stimulating.
Have some interesting life experience.
Enjoy travel, especially faraway places with an exotic flair.
Be spontaneous, ready for adventure at any moment.
Share his passion for life, experience, and discovery.
Finish a graduate degree (or at least be well read).
Be permissive and open-minded.
Allow him his time with "the guys."
Allow him solo travel (good for his mind).
Cultivate your spiritual side.
Be up-to-date on world affairs.
Flirt with attractive men.
Keep him guessing.
Know how to enjoy life.

DON'T

Press for commitment.
Be possessive and clingy.
Put out his fire with cynical thinking.
Be narrow-minded or provincial.
Be overly formal (in dress or attitude).
Be unfair or unreasonable.
Blindly accept whatever he says.

Neglect the environment.
Impose limits, restraints, and rules.
Get too emotional on him.
Be available every time he calls.
Stop learning or discovering.
Make a jealous scene if he flirts with other girls.
Become some sort of burden on him.
Be just one of his gals.

BEST WAYS TO IMPRESS

Be fluent in a foreign language (the more exotic, the better).
Have dual citizenship.
Be a personal friend of the Dalai Lama.
Have several Ph.D.'s.
Have your own airplane.

BEST WAYS TO GET DUMPED

Tell him you hate flying.
Be a party pooper.
Steal his passport.
Announce that your biological clock is ticking.
Press for marriage after your first date.

FASHION

The Sag man is not especially fashion-savvy. Unaware of the current trends, he just thinks a woman should look "good." And clothes should never restrict bodily movement, or make running impossible. If anything, they should enable a woman to express her freedom, both physically and spiritually.

Because of his passion for foreign countries, he might especially appreciate pieces or fabrics from far-off lands. And he also enjoys some novelty and fun stuff. But he's not into the formal look, especially for daytime or a fun night out—he could be perfectly tickled by "dressed-up jeans" or a sexy (yet wearable) dress. And since he really appreciates a good set of thighs, those girls who have them should flaunt them.

As for accessories, it's the same story. The Sag man could probably care less if you sport the latest fad. And any bags or bracelets inspired by other cultures (or purchased abroad) would make more of an impact than those made in the United States. Maybe the only must-have is a set of nice travel bags. And your cosmetic case doesn't have to be huge, just big enough for some lip gloss and suntan lotion.

GIFT IDEAS: Those that are foreign, athletic, spiritual, or mind-opening

BEER BUDGET

Tickets to his favorite sporting event
Outdoor wear
Baseball cap
Foreign-language CDs
Atlas
Compass

CHAMPAGNE BUDGET

Deluxe sleeping bag
Airfare to Tahiti
Sturdy luggage
Encyclopedia set
Ancient artifact
Private jet

ADD SOME SPICE

Some spice can only make things more interesting. Feel free to season generously.

Some Ideas

1. Take a class on some obscure subject he knows nothing about so you can have an edge over him.
2. Take off to the other side of the world, be inaccessible, then return to flaunt your adventures.
3. Get drunk and play strip poker.
4. Join the boys in the cigar bar to prove you can puff in high heels.

IF YOU SENSE A LOOMING BREAKUP

It won't be easy to know when the Sag man is looking for a break, because he's not exclusive and clingy in the first place. And because a good-bye means new freedom, he won't be all gloomy and dark in the days preceding a breakup. He's just an optimistic person in general, so he could sport a big smile at the same time he's planning his escape. But he's pretty direct, too, so he might just spill the beans before you have time to assess the situation. Still, there may be behavioral changes to watch for if you start to bore him.

Danger Signs to Watch For

- More time with the boys
- More solo travel
- More drinking and partying
- Less one-on-one contact
- Even more open flirting
- Lunches with ex-girlfriends—or new girl "friends"
- Increasing restlessness

If you're sure things are drawing to an end, don't panic or overreact. The worst thing you could do is go to him with an emotional breakdown. Or beg. Maybe the best thing to do would be to disappear out of his life, suddenly and quickly, while changing your telephone number and e-mail address. Let him hear about you through the grapevine—all about your fun pursuits and sexy guy friends. Or take off to Africa and send him a postcard from your great safari trip (and a picture of your foreign lover). Impress him by having the courage to start over again. He might realize you're one in a million and bounce back into your life when you least suspect it.

For those gals who hate playing games, the best approach to an impending ending is an open and friendly one. The Sagittarius man is usually direct, so the truth should come out quickly. His most likely argument in favor of a breakup is a lack of freedom or readiness for a committed relationship. And there's not much you can say to that, so set him free and wish him luck in the big world. Just make it clear that you're "broken up" if he wants to rekindle the fire at a future date. Unless he comes back with some sort of commitment, another "fun moment" is probably a waste of time.

AND NEVER FORGET

His essential need to explore and learn

HOW MR. SAGITTARIUS SEES YOU

	AT BEST	AT WORST
Aries	independent, courageous	demanding, selfish
Taurus	sensual, natural	possessive, grounded
Gemini	versatile, fun	nervous, dissipated
Cancer	genial, feminine	cautious, brooding
Leo	generous, warm	demanding, elitist

Virgo	tempering, healthy	prudent, reserved
Libra	fair, tolerant	dependent, sophisticated
Scorpio	exciting, daring	consuming, possessive
Sagittarius	happy, adventurous	sisterly, overly eager
Capricorn	wise, stabilizing	narrow-minded, cold
Aquarius	liberal, unique	stubborn, cool
Pisces	adaptable, idealistic	complex, lazy

COUPLES COMPATIBILITY

BEST BETS	WHY NOT?	CHALLENGING
Aquarius	Libra	Capricorn
Gemini	Pisces	Cancer
Aries	Scorpio	Taurus
Leo		Virgo
Sagittarius		

SAGITTARIUS MAN (Steven Spielberg) and SCORPIO WOMAN (Kate Capshaw)

These two signs have little in common, but they can work together if their best qualities (and not their worst) dominate. We all know that the Sag man is really a *big boy* at heart. And big boys are enthusiastic but not always pragmatic. If this guy learns to channel his energy into truly productive pursuits (rather than waste it here and there and everywhere), he can gain the admiration of the Scorpio woman, who will stand by her man as he pulls off one amazing feat after another. But if his mission in life is simply to have a good time, the intensity of Ms. Scorpio's love will fade—and quickly. Now, to keep her Sag man happy, she'll have to learn to *trust* him. And to be a good sport. And to let go sometimes. "If you love someone, set them free"—these are wise words for a Scorpio woman in love with a

Sagittarius man. And if Mr. Sag realizes how lucky he is to be hooked up to such a strong and passionate woman, the kind who can temper his blind optimism with a little realism and intuition, he should be back for good.

SOME ADVICE—TAKE IT OR LEAVE IT

YOUR SIGN	
Aries	DO: share his enthusiasm for the latest plan DON'T: give him orders
Taurus	DO: indulge in your mutual love of food and nature DON'T: fence him in or tie him down
Gemini	DO: share his love of travel and exploration DON'T: get caught up in the trivial matters of the moment
Cancer	DO: get him to stay around by offering him great food and wine DON'T: engulf him in your dark moods
Leo	DO: delight him with your zesty appetite for life DON'T: play the role of prima donna
Virgo	DO: research topics, cultures, and hobbies that interest him DON'T: nag if he wants to have a little too much fun
Libra	DO: employ your talent to see life from his perspective DON'T: pout when he leaves you alone
Scorpio	DO: explore your innate love of adventure DON'T: scare him off with your jealousy and need to control
Sagittarius	DO: have great fun playing around with each other DON'T: become too much of a buddy
Capricorn	DO: let him bring out the kid in you DON'T: alienate him with your harsh view of the world
Aquarius	DO: delight him with your novel ideas and mutual need for space DON'T: chill his bubbling optimism with your dispassion
Pisces	DO: use your imagination to plan romantic escapades and travels DON'T: get all depressed for no reason

Looking Farther Down the Road

TRUE LOVE

THE ENGAGEMENT

The chances of getting a marriage proposal out of this carefree commitment-phobe are slightly greater than holding the winning Lotto ticket. But it could happen to you! A lot depends on timing and luck. If your Sagittarius guy is still young, he probably isn't ready for a confining relationship like marriage—chances are he needs more years to explore and learn and get the traveling bug out of his system. But if he's in his forties, say, and if his friends are all married and have kids, he might start feeling left out (and lonely) and venture to take a step into the Marriage Zone.

Just never resort to nasty ultimatums and manipulation to get a proposal. Your Sag man will have a great excuse to make a break if you use underhanded tactics to pressure him. Maybe the best approach is a philosophical one. Make marriage seem like another life experience, one to be tried, at least. Or present it as some sort of daring challenge (just to make it sound more exciting). But don't wait *too* long. If years go by without any reference to a deeper commitment, keep him as a friend and move on. It's even possible (but not probable) that the minute you go solo is the minute he accepts the challenge of a long-term relationship. You never know.

THE WEDDING

Now that you have some sort of commitment, don't disappoint him by making a huge fuss over the wedding. Remember, this is supposed to seem fun and exciting, not dreary and serious. And think twice before rejecting one of his more daring or spontaneous plans, like popping off to Vegas for a quickie wedding. Unless you're a die-hard wedding freak, you'd better stay open-minded and tolerant in the wedding process. And there's no need to get all formal or businesslike—you'd only scare him off.

The most important thing is that a good mood prevail at the wedding, however you decide to celebrate it. And an abundance of food and drink is a must—nothing could be less auspicious to future happiness and growth than a miserly or spartan affair. This is a day to rejoice, and nothing, not even a hurricane, should ruin it for you. The philosophical Sag man knows how to make the best of every moment, so don't worry and be happy.

THE HONEYMOON

Here's the event your Sag man has been waiting for (and it may be one of his main reasons for enduring that wedding thing in the first place). Chances are he's already made far-reaching plans, but in case he's floundering, help plan a honeymoon that rivals all other trips. And invest in all the travel accessories that could make the trip even more successful.

The best thing you could do is keep this adventure exciting and interesting. If you go to a far-off land, be open to immersing yourself in the culture. Try incorporating some of the local or religious customs into your agenda, just to make the trip that much more authentic. If you go to a more ordinary place, plan fun activities like scuba diving or bungee jumping. This trip is your first one in wedlock and will set the mood for the months to come. Don't let married life equal boring life. Make him wish he'd tied the knot with you years ago.

Honeymoon Sex

"Legal" sex is a new concept to him, so surprise your Sag man by making it a mind-blower. Try incorporating the sexual customs of the spot you're in, just to make it more interesting. Or dare to make love in the most unlikely of places, like a cave, a tree, or a jungle. Keep it thrilling and adventurous, but don't expect sex day and night. Your hubby may be too wrapped up in his new habitat and too thirsty for new discoveries to want it all the time.

MAKING IT IN THE LONG HAUL

Don't make the mistake of becoming smug now that you're hitched. If you want to hold your Sag hubby for the long term, you'll have the formidable challenge of keeping married life spicy and interesting. If your marriage is on the same page next year, you're in trouble. Leave options open and be ready for the next dare. Keep up with your Sag man and evolve at the same rate. And leave him plenty of free time for nights out with "the boys." Don't let him lose that wonderful smile of his. And don't lose yours, either.

DOS AND DON'TS FOR LASTING BLISS

DO

Add some spontaneity to daily life.
Continue to make new and interesting friends.
Plan lots of travel time.
Learn a foreign language.
Take some interesting night classes.
Let your home be open to his friends.

Attend social and sporting events.
Be enthusiastic about his latest plan or idea.
Be open to changes of residence (even countries).
Allow him to flirt with other gals.
Stay open-minded and farsighted.
Know how to enjoy yourself.
Dare to face the unknown.
Give him lots of physical affection.
Experiment with exotic recipes.
Know how to guide him when he's a bit lost.

DON'T

Make life dreary and boring.
Mock his idealistic goals.
Grow cynical and bitter with age.
Scold him for being childish.
Lose that sparkle in your eye.
Grow old and be unable to keep up with him.
Keep him locked inside the house.
Exacerbate his restlessness with your own instability.
Ever stop exploring and evolving.
Demand drawn-out romantic overtures before sex.
Develop a severe outlook on life.
Refuse to entertain his friends.
Alienate him by becoming a super-snob.
Let him be Mr. Know-It-All-All-the-Time.
Get depressed and lose your taste for life.

EARTHLY BLISS (AKA SEX)

The Sag man has a big appetite for life and all its trappings, so sex must satisfy. More important, sex must satisfy *over the long term* to keep your hubby fully engaged. Spontaneity and adventure will always save the day, and varied times and positions will add some fun, too. Just don't let a demanding job sap all your energy and leave your Sag man in a cold bed. You must be up and ready when he is (even if you're dying to get some sleep).

Sex is not such an emotional act for your Sag man, so don't put out his fire with a whole list of pre-sex demands (like demanding he bear his soul or recite all the reasons he loves you). Sex should be fun and unconditional. This guy also hates duties and obligations, so never make sex with you feel like a "chore."

If your sex life begins to lag, be open and ask him what he wants. If it's a new kick, indulge him. If it's more excitement, seduce him when he's least suspecting (like in a stopped elevator on his way to a staff meeting). There's never an excuse to get in a rut, so keep sex thrilling and lively.

AND CHEATING . . . ?

If you must know, the Sag man is one of the more likely men to fool around. Not because he doesn't love you, but because he craves variety, excitement, and women. But he wouldn't risk a dangerous liaison if he thought you'd find out and suffer, because the last thing he wants is to cause you pain. His philosophy is more along the lines of "What you don't know can't hurt you." Unfortunately, he's not very discreet, and is rather distracted, so chances are you'd find out sooner rather than later, unless it's just a one-night fling in a far-off place. (And if he does travel out of state or overseas often, you can be sure that he has some *very* friendly dinner company, at the very least.)

Of course, not all Sag men are unfaithful, especially if they're the more bookish or spiritual type. But the bon vivant Sagittarius man, who loves drinking, gambling, and girls, can be a real womanizer, swooning over one delectable creature after another.

(Luckily, this is also the type of Sag man who doesn't often marry, so you're probably not in a relationship with this one, anyway.)

The best thing you can do to prevent any extracurricular activity is to maintain your sex appeal and delicious personality. Let him see how appealing his friends find you (and how thrilled they'd be to get you in bed). Don't ever let him think he has you under his thumb, and throw some curveballs at him from time to time. If you do catch him in a blunder, confront him amusingly, then challenge him to sleep with three more girls by week's end. Be "above" jealousy, make his goofs look petty and "unevolved," and take the fun out of his girl-chasing. (Just *never* become desperate and pathetic, or he'll lose all respect for you.) Yes, it will take lots of games to keep this guy in line, but that's the fun of it. And if you simply can't cope, don't marry him in the first place.

REASONS HE MIGHT CHEAT

- If he meets an attractive foreigner abroad
- If he's trying to show off to "the boys"
- If he meets a girl who will take him to another horizon
- If he just wants to have a little fun

WHAT YOU CAN DO

- Continue to learn so you can be every woman to him.
- Intrigue him by changing your look and attitude.
- Let him see how fascinating his friends find you.
- Keep him on his toes with unexpected behavior.
- Compliment him on being so evolved (wink, wink!).
- Don't pass if he asks you to join him on a trip.

SOME THINGS TO TWEAK

One of the reasons the Sag man is interesting is because of his insatiable hunger for new experiences. On the other hand, it's also one of the reasons he remains forever restless and dissatisfied. Point out to him that the most interesting things in life are not necessarily the most exotic and unattainable ones. And let him know that what he's looking for might actually be on his doorstep. He loves to read, so set up a home library with subjects like travel, religion, spirituality, and philosophy. Encourage him to travel in his mind, not just his body. Although he doesn't know it, what he really needs is inner tranquillity. Try to get him interested in yoga or tai chi. If there's one man who can benefit from such activities, it's your Sag husband, who's open to any mind- and body-enhancing experience.

Then you might want to help him curb some of his excesses and strive for a little more moderation. This guy can really overdo it in the food, drink, athletic, gambling, or sex departments, living as though there's no tomorrow. Some might support this philosophy, and to some extent it is rather positive. Still, he might well live till a hundred, so he wouldn't want to burn through his physical or financial resources by fifty. Besides, this careless behavior doesn't really jibe with some of the "loftier" ideas he trumpets to the rest of us primates, so maybe we're seeing something of a hypocrite here. Get him to take notice of his contradictions and help him achieve a more balanced life if he goes overboard.

AND HAPPILY EVER AFTER . . .

Who said life has to be a drag? Not your Sag man. And you'd better not let him think of you as a burden if you want to keep him under your roof. Just be a willing partner in exploring new horizons (mental and/or physical), and married life should stay rosy. Sure, you might not always be in the mood to cross the Sahara on camelback, so set him free if he's jumping out of his pants. Don't worry, he'll be back to brag. And maybe you'll join him on the next adventure. There are more interesting things to do in life than staying home and knitting, so stop being a granny and start living—you'll have plenty of time for bedrest when you're ninety.

Capricorn, the Goat

(about December 22 till about January 20)

Feel the temperature dropping? You might when the Capricorn man trudges into your life. This old goat is determined to make it to the top of the mountain, in the face of great obstacles, even if it means ignoring his heart. So before you go after this man, understand that love comes second to career and status, which is why many a Goat stays single for a long time. Still, there is hope. Ever heard the saying "Behind every great man stands a great woman"? Probably coined by a Capricorn man, and it's precisely this type of woman who may get him.

The Goat is known to be cold, sometimes ruthless, but he's not heartless. Still, there's something "heavy" about his presence, as though years of burden and responsibility have taken their toll. He's the kind of guy you want to tell, "Lighten up—life's not *that* bad!" But he might not be able to see life from your point of view, and his priorities are probably different. The Goat is convinced (maybe wrongly) that success will bring him the happiness he desires, and his path toward achievement leaves little place for sentimentality and emotions that can hinder his ability to think and act. But be assured there is a tender, beating heart under that coat of arms, one that will eventually open up to the right girl.

The key to attracting this man is to make him realize you would be an asset, not a liability, to him. Being a great hostess, knowing how to make contacts with influential people, agreeing to entertain boring business partners or potential investors, dressing for success, being part of the right groups—these are traits that are important to him when choosing a partner. The Goat likes women who have great careers themselves or, if they don't work, belong to important social clubs or organizations. This is not the guy whose dream is to come home to the wife who sits around all day while the noisy and disobedient kids make a mess of the house. No way! This man wants a woman who will do everything in her power to build him up and see to it that his ambitious goals are achieved. If you're already hesitating, consider the fruits to be enjoyed after years of hard work. Great things take years to happen but have long-lasting benefits.

Not surprisingly, the Capricorn man is often attracted to girls from rich or powerful families (it sure wouldn't hurt to be the President's niece or, better yet, daughter), not because he's a social climber (well, maybe a little bit), but simply because he's drawn to power and influence. In reality, though, it usually suffices that a girl is motivated and ambitious. Still, what the Goat *really* needs, without realizing it, is a woman who can warm him up with love and affection. A driven but selfish woman can't do much for him in the happiness department, so what's the point in the long term? The ideal woman would be equally ambitious and affectionate, and this is the type of female the Goat could eventually respect and love. (And if the Goat is already older and well-established, he has less need for an ambitious woman and more need for a young and lovely one.)

But as with everything worthwhile, a relationship with this

man takes *time*. He's not the type to dive headfirst into a relationship without knowing precisely the kind of girl he's dealing with. A random girl he meets in a bar will be suspect (unless she does happen to be the President's daughter). The Goat believes in a certain protocol when it comes to dating, and prefers to meet potential partners through trusted friends, colleagues, or family members. If a certain girl is able to inspire a spark, the cautious Goat will patiently gather information about her and take one step at a time to ensure that he does not make a bad judgment. No, this guy is certainly not the romantic fool, but a mature man with an agenda.

When a Capricorn man starts dating, he takes his responsibilities seriously (yes, even a relationship becomes a responsibility to him). And, eventually, there's a good feeling, but never fireworks. It doesn't mean he doesn't like you, it just means he has a different way to show it. So don't fret if your Goat doesn't jump with joy each time he sees you—he's just being himself. And sometimes that means playing the sober, protective father-type instead of the dashing playboy or tormented artist.

As you get to know him, though, you'll see that he can be really funny, in a way that others can't. And he has

THE CAPRICORN MAN IS

AT BEST	AT WORST
Patient	Slow
Hardworking	Inhibited
Mature	Stiff
Persevering	Narrow-Minded
Ambitious	Ruthless
Responsible	Calculating
Reliable	Dull
Loyal	Cold
Humorous	Cynical
Lawful	Pessimistic
Traditional	Ultraconservative
Stable	Harsh
Economical	Stingy
Cautious	Opportunistic
Wise	Melancholic
Productive	Solitary

great timing—just when things are going their worst, he can lighten up the situation with his unique sense of humor. If you're lucky enough to be around when he's in this mind-set, enjoy the moment and show your delight. Laughter is great for everyone, but critical for this man, who tends to view life too seriously. Think about taking him out to some funny movies or encouraging him to wind down with intimate but amusing friends. Even something as simple as a smile could cheer him up, so don't think you have to be serious just because he is.

Though you may suffer a bit with this man in the short term, you'll appreciate him more and more as your relationship deepens (and especially after the age of forty, when he really starts to enjoy life). Don't let him fool you into believing he cannot love, because he can, and very deeply. Nothing will happen quickly with this man, not in life and not in romance, but a slow and steady advance is almost assured, and if you are patient and know how to stand behind him and build him up, you will be rewarded with a loyal and constant heart.

SOME FAMOUS CAPRICORN MEN

Nicolas Cage, Mel Gibson, Val Kilmer, Jude Law, Tiger Woods, Jim Carrey, Anthony Hopkins, Denzel Washington, Cary Grant, Al Capone, David Bowie, Richard Nixon, Woodrow Wilson, Jon Voight, Kevin Costner, Rod Stewart, Louis Pasteur, Mohammed Ali, George Foreman, Howard Hughes, Elvis Presley, Edgar Allan Poe, Benjamin Franklin, Ralph Fiennes

MUST HAVE BEEN A CAPRICORN MAN

Edward Lewis *(Pretty Woman)* (But only in Hollywood would this Goat date a hooker!)

THE SEDUCTION

The Goat doesn't have much time for love, so he's not usually on the lookout in an everyday scenario. The best place to get him to notice you is at the office, a dinner party, or any place he frequents. Probably the first thing that might intrigue him is your posture and attitude (oh, and your expensive-looking wardrobe). He takes quick notice of "important people," so a confident woman who knows her value might pique his interest. It's no secret that he's impressed by authentic beauty, though, as in great bone structure and beautiful teeth, so if you happen to have a Christy Turlington smile, don't hesitate to show it.

Still, this man won't dash up to you to ask you out, no matter how much you appeal to him. Instead, he'll take time to check up on you or inquire about your reputation. If he discovers a woman has slept with the entire office, he'll avoid her like the plague. But if he learns she is someone to be respected, he could plan his next move.

Because he's cautious in affairs of the heart, he usually trusts a girl who is equally prudent. If he finally asks you out for a date, insist that he be on time, pick you up at your house, tell you where you are going beforehand and what time you'll be back. (This is one guy you can even present to your parents or siblings on date number one.) Don't be discouraged by the lack of instant fire, because the Goat needs a lot of time to warm up—at least you don't have to worry about him trying to lure you back to his home on the first date (and if he does try, be aware that it might be a test!).

You'll probably go through a traditional courting period if you're with one of the more typical Goats. After a strong bond has been established (which could take a long time), you might want to loosen him up with a bit of champagne and encourage the advances he's been thinking about making. Just don't sleep with him too soon or he'll think you're too fast and easy. When you do finally decide it's the moment, make sure you have total privacy and keep the sex normal—that means no whips and chains with this old Goat!

SEX

conservative, slow, earthy, good

Believe it or not, the Goat really enjoys sex. He might be inhibited in the beginning, but when he feels very close to a woman, he can summon his low-key passion and really go at it. Don't forget, some Goats are horned Rams, with an above-average sex drive (and some women claim they are among the best in bed). Still, in general, he's not like a ticking time bomb waiting to go off, so he might not seem that eager. In fact, he's got a lot more self-control than some other animals out there, and this might be good news for some women.

He's probably at his best under the right circumstances, like in a very private setting with dimmed lights. This type of atmosphere also enables him to let himself go (well, as much as he can), since there's zero risk of exposure. It would be a big waste of time to seduce him in a public rest room—it's just not his style (and he'd probably despise you for trying). He believes there's a certain protocol for everything, so sex should transpire on a bed, at least in the beginning.

And sex should always remain a private affair. He'd really be upset to learn that your sex life is a topic of conversation on Girls' Night Out. This is serious stuff, he thinks, not the subject matter of frivolous gossip. Besides, he has a reputation to uphold, so it wouldn't do to let his pants down before the entire world.

DOS AND DON'TS OF A GREAT RELATIONSHIP

DO

Be motivated and ambitious.
Know your etiquette.
Be affectionate and loving.
Show him you are hardworking.
Respect tradition, rules, and laws.
Know the value of money (and good investment strategies).
Know how to make the right friends.
Help him hone his strategy.
Allow him overtime work hours.
Cultivate an interest in politics or antiques.
Try to earn brownie points with his boss or potential employers.
Be ready to entertain when necessary.
Try to brighten his day with a smile.
Have clearly defined long-term goals.
Be groomed and presentable, all the time.

DON'T

Be overly sentimental.
Be a self-pitying loser.
Waste time and money.
Be irresponsible and careless.
Show flagrant disrespect for authority and rules.
Demand passionate displays of love.
Associate with the wrong people.
Push him to make rash decisions.
Waste any potential you have.
Showcase self-destructive behavior.
Neglect your appearance and home.
Make enemies with men or women in power.

Make unreasonable demands that are not in his interest.
Partake in scandalous behavior that could affect his situation in the future.
Give him reason to think you'd be a liability to him in any way.

BEST WAYS TO IMPRESS

Have connections to the White House.
Have an important father.
Be an Ivy League graduate with fantastic contacts.
Be a *genuine* beauty.
Make the cover of *Town & Country*.

BEST WAYS TO GET DUMPED

Lose your job and become a couch potato.
Get thrown into jail and make the six o'clock news.
Run naked through the city.
Tell him you're a swinger.

FASHION

Appearance is capital for the Capricorn man, who favors prestige dressing, or clothes that say, "I'm someone." Even the Goat who is less worldly has respect for people who pay attention to the way they present themselves. In any case, the aspiring Goat admires women with quality clothes—you know, perfect cuts, expensive fabrics, and a timeless quality. And he has absolutely nothing against the most prestigious designer clothes. But don't get the impression that he only admires conservative clothes—not true. A very feminine dress or slightly sexy ensemble could do wonders for his psyche under the right circumstances (but not when you are dining with his boss's wife, who is twenty years older!). It's up to you to know what's appropriate and when.

What's really funny is how impressed he is by the great fashion houses. Because he's so into names, the real Capricorn man would prefer his girlfriend wear a not-so-flattering dress from one of the greats than a stunning handmade outfit. (But he wouldn't find anything amusing about a forty-five-year-old woman sporting trendy teeny-bopper wear, even if it was designer.) And he's not especially romantic, so he'd opt for an entire outfit straight off a window mannequin over one that dares some artistic experimentation (probably because the latter has a higher chance of failure).

Still, most of us women actually have a budget, so it's fortunate to know that any well-studied outfit that won't cause a scandal should do just fine. If money is lacking, a wise woman would buy clothes in "expensive" colors like black, beige, and camel, which always make an outfit seem more costly than it is.

Thank God for Louis Vuitton and Hermès that Capricorn men abound! This is the man who'll encourage his girlfriend to have all the designer accessories, just so everyone knows she's "important." Not only the bags and shoes, but the key chains, sunglasses, wallets, attaché, and all the rest. The Goat likes things to match, so he might be loyal to one house just so the textures or colors go together. Anyway, the Goat loves when a woman's shoes match her purse and belt and scarf, and things like that, so it'll take some special planning to please this one. And let's not forget his great appreciation for diamonds and precious stones (or maybe you've heard enough already).

GIFT IDEAS: Those that scream "status"! Otherwise, gifts that are useful or can aid him on his path to success.

BEER BUDGET

Sterling-silver picture frame
Reference computer software (e.g., estate planning, law, architecture)
Famous opera arias CD
Books (politics, art history, satire, memoirs)
Polo shirt
Calendar (with daily proverbs or jokes)

CHAMPAGNE BUDGET

Designer tie and matching pocket scarf
Case of expensive champagne
Designer luggage
Membership to elite gym
Antique furniture
Limousine and chauffeur

ADD SOME SPICE

There may be times when you're dying to serve up some hot sauce, but the conservative Goat wouldn't suffer lightly a case of heartburn. Some mild herbs would suit him better.

Some Ideas

1. Have his secretary postpone a couple meetings so you can seduce him out of his rigorous routine.
2. Give him a full-body massage and see where it leads to.
3. Surprise him with a weekend away at a romantic five-star hotel.
4. Wear a sexy apron and stilettos while whipping up a gourmet candlelight dinner for two.

IF YOU SENSE A LOOMING BREAKUP

Figuring out if your Goat is unhappy in love won't be easy, because he's not the cheeriest man to begin with. You may find it hard to determine whether his gloom is due to his genetic character or to romantic misgivings. And an unfulfilled Goat might postpone bad news until after an important business project, so you could wait in suspense for months. Take it upon yourself to figure out his intentions so you can make your own plans to try to reverse things.

Danger Signs to Watch For

- More time at work and less time for you
- Growing coldness or fatigue
- Increasingly harsh words or criticism
- More solo outings and travel
- Decreasing investment of time and money in you
- Less approval of you and your lifestyle

If you're convinced he's falling out of love, it's pretty serious, because he's not a frivolous person who falls in and out of love ten times a day. Actually, the Goat is quite calculating, so you can almost bet his change of heart isn't spontaneous or temporary. But he's reasonable, so it might not be a bad idea to confront him directly, in a cool and calm way. If you really want to keep him, you might have to let him go for a while so he has time to live alone or date other women. In the meantime, it wouldn't hurt to plunge into your work and make great professional strides he is sure to hear about. And it wouldn't be a bad idea to date a VIP. Your Goat will only admire a resilient woman who can fend for herself in this world, so prove you're made of the right stuff if you ever hope for a reconciliation.

But if your Capricorn boyfriend is convinced that there's no future together, then there's no use in discussing anything. And once he's made up his mind to end a relationship, he can do it curtly and officially and, to tell you the truth, quite easily. This man has the amazing ability to harden his heart when he needs to, and the last thing he'd do is get all emotional and teary-eyed over a good-bye. It must be some sort of protective mechanism that kicks in at the right moment, but it's always there when he needs it, even in the love department. So don't think your own tears and feelings will wear him down—if anything, they'll just make him pity you. If he dumps you, just move on and *get a life*—that would make more of an impact than making a scene. Besides, you wouldn't want to let him think he was that important to you in the first place.

AND NEVER FORGET

His essential need to achieve

HOW MR. CAPRICORN SEES YOU

	AT BEST	AT WORST
Aries	ambitious, dynamic	impulsive, tough
Taurus	realistic, affectionate	self-indulgent, jealous
Gemini	rejuvenating, rational	inconstant, silly
Cancer	prudent, supportive	needy, emotionally messy
Leo	dignified, status-conscious	extravagant, dramatic
Virgo	practical, hardworking	anxious, pessimistic
Libra	diplomatic, classy	flittering, self-indulgent
Scorpio	driven, strong	rebellious, vulgar
Sagittarius	uplifting, lucky	irresponsible, adventurous
Capricorn	ambitious, realistic	unaffectionate, melancholic
Aquarius	helpful, well-connected	nonconformist, eccentric
Pisces	supportive, tender	irrational, bohemian

COUPLES COMPATIBILITY

BEST BETS	WHY NOT?	CHALLENGING
Taurus	Libra	Aquarius
Scorpio	Aries	Pisces
Leo	Sagittarius	Gemini
Virgo		Capricorn
Cancer		

CAPRICORN MAN (David Bowie) and LEO WOMAN (Iman)

Different energy, but a strong couple! The sunny warmth of a Leo woman is just what a Capricorn man needs to lift him out of his doldrums. And Mr. Capricorn admires the Leo woman, because she's usually of the winning breed. Not only is she good in everything she does, but Ms. Leo has a public image her Capricorn lover can be proud of. And she has a knack for raising children in a responsible and productive manner. It's true the Leo woman can have a big idea of herself and expect special treatment, but that's okay for the Capricorn man, who admires people with self-respect and high self-esteem, anyway. As for her, Ms. Leo should have every reason to stay with her Capricorn man, who's more an "establishment" type than a fly-by-night one. Who else could maintain her lavish lifestyle? If he's equally ambitious in bed, these success-oriented people make a winning team that could last for decades.

SOME ADVICE—TAKE IT OR LEAVE IT

YOUR SIGN	
Aries	Do: warm him up with your fire and steer him toward success Don't: be so impatient and short-winded
Taurus	Do: endear youself to him with your respect for money and long-term thinking Don't: insist he join you when you're in the mood to be lazy
Gemini	Do: get connected to people who could help him Don't: make promises you can't keep
Cancer	Do: tell him your intuitive feelings to help him make decisions Don't: bog him down with your excessive emotions
Leo	Do: be the noble woman he can be proud of Don't: snub his colleagues or people he needs
Virgo	Do: some of the dirty work to aid him in his ascension Don't: dwell on the negatives and make him even more pessimistic
Libra	Do: be the gracious host you can be and know how to charm the boss Don't: expect him to go out and play all the time
Scorpio	Do: use your energy to help him realize his goals Don't: do anything that will ruin his or your reputation
Sagittarius	Do: infuse him with some of your optimism and zest for life Don't: exaggerate your wanderlust and need for adventure
Capricorn	Do: bring some fun and laughter into your lives Don't: exacerbate his already harsh view of reality
Aquarius	Do: help him make the right contacts Don't: shock him with your radical or progressive thinking
Pisces	Do: use your tenderness to lure him out of his armor Don't: prove to be too weak to cope with life

Looking Farther Down the Road

TRUE LOVE

THE ENGAGEMENT

A marriage proposal won't happen overnight, not with this Goat. He needs to be *sure* you're the woman who will make a good life partner, and that could take a long time. Besides, he needs to be convinced he's even ready for the next step. Until he's a bit older or well-established in his professional life, marriage won't be thinkable (unless he finds a woman who can bring instant benefit to his situation). But he respects the institution of marriage and plans to settle down one of these days. Just be careful not to appall him with uncivilized or scandalous behavior—he could drop you like a brick, even after years of serious dating.

If time goes by with no hint about the future, you might need to give him a little push. Tell him you have big plans in life, and if he's not the man to share them with, you'd like to find someone else. Or appeal to his sense of protocol and remind him that a woman is expected to marry by a certain time (an outdated notion to many people, but not to this traditional man). Just stay mellow and sweet. Your Capricorn man can easily recognize words of wisdom. If he asks for a little more time, be reasonable. But don't give him years.

THE WEDDING

You'll need to put all your energy into perfect planning, because the Goat would be shamed by a botched-up party. And play it safe—that means no experimental wedding scenarios, like marrying in a swimming pool. He'd be relieved to know you were working with a prestigious or well-reputed wedding planner, so consider one if you can afford it. Just don't go bothering your husband-to-be with daily questions—he has a job to do. Assure him that your wedding will be a success so he can sleep at night.

You should think tradition and quality when making the plans—the correct invitations (sent out on time), the perfect menu, the corresponding wines (the older, the better), the right guests (you know what that means to him), the appropriate music. Buy a book on wedding etiquette if you must. Just make sure there are no unpleasant surprises or obnoxious guests—this day must be a crowning achievement.

THE HONEYMOON

Your Capricorn man will probably take care of all the honeymoon plans, because it's the groom's traditional "obligation." But if he's been too busy working, find the time to plan a successful trip yourself. And don't economize on travel plans. Even though he's wise with his money, he usually likes to travel first-class so the whole world knows he's "made it." And if there's one vacation he'll want to splurge on, it's this one.

Provided the wedding was a success, your Capricorn man will finally exhale and enjoy the honeymoon. Just be sure to keep him happy, not only with a sweet disposition but with a well-planned trip. That means knowing your travel etiquette, the sites to see, the exclusive restaurants, and basic communication in case you find yourself lost in some strange country. Encourage your Goat to loosen up and forget about the "harsh world." Just don't take this trip for granted—it won't come around again.

Honeymoon Sex

Don't be surprised if your Capricorn man carries you over the threshold! He might just think it's the thing to do, since he's seen it in so many movies. Anyway, there's only one way to make love for the first time as a married couple—the traditional way. So don your new white nightgown (and matching slippers) and reach for the champagne. Your Goat will take things from there.

MAKING IT IN THE LONG HAUL

This is your long-haul man, so be grateful to know that life will get easier with time. Once the house is decorated, the friends are made, and the career is stable, your Capricorn man should learn to relax a bit more and enjoy life (well, as much as he can). To endear yourself to him forever, continue to be productive, know how to run a responsible household, and support him in his quest to achieve while managing to soften his edges with your loving touch. You've gotten this far, so don't mess it up now—the best of your Goat is still to come.

DOS AND DON'TS FOR LASTING BLISS

DO

Know how to dress for success.
Continue making friends with people who could be useful to him.
Perfect your social etiquette.
Know how to coddle him when he's had a rough day.
Bring laughter into the home.
Show him respect, in public and private.
Demand value for your money.

Take good care of your home, furnishings, and cars.
Offer him regular compliments (on his suit, his haircut, etc.).
Join an exclusive golf, tennis, or country club.
Inspire him to dream from time to time.
See him through his pessimistic periods.
Reassure him of your devotion and love.
Get him to take a day off from time to time.
Be the wife he can be proud of.

DON'T

Start boozing or engage in other reckless behavior.
Sleep in till noon.
Get yourselves into debt.
Antagonize authority figures and make enemies.
Sit around and watch soaps all day.
Live for celebrity gossip.
Get involved in any sort of potential scandal.
Scold him for long work hours.
Rattle him with ultimatums and scenes.
Let his serious moods melt your smile.
Wreak havoc on his professional life.
Let him come home to a big mess.
Complain if he cancels a date for a business meeting.
Indulge in frivolous and wasteful shopping sprees.
Neglect your children (or his).

EARTHLY BLISS (AKA SEX)

Sex is an important way for your Capricorn man to de-stress. Yes, he might be tired after a long day's work, and there will be periods when he just can't find the time, but when he's ready for some loving, he'll count on your body to warm him up.

Unlike some other men out there, the Goat usually enjoys conjugal sex more and more as the years roll by. And he might look forward to post-sex discussions in bed, when he's relaxed enough to talk over his problems and concerns. He probably wouldn't appreciate you jumping out of bed to run errands after a half hour of pleasure—this is the time to give him a good massage and a sympathetic ear.

As for the sex itself, you shouldn't be too worried about keeping it interesting. Quality counts, so try making it deeper and more satisfying each time. And don't act shocked if he ever proposes something unique—he might be looking for the ultimate satisfaction. Just never make fun of him if he wants to try something new. And never criticize his performance. This man is sensitive deep down inside and will recoil the second you make him feel awkward or ridiculous. It all comes down to this: The Capricorn man wants *respect,* in the bedroom as well as the boardroom.

AND CHEATING . . . ?

Even though the Goat might lust after an attractive woman, he's not a risk-taker and won't easily get involved in an affair that could compromise his reputation and situation. Besides, he's not the romantic swooner anyway and has more important things to do with his time than make a fool out of himself. Still, if he ever reaches a point of power where he thinks anything is permissible, he would be capable of sleeping with another woman. He figures, "Presidents do it, why shouldn't I?" It would be more likely a result of a power trip than animalistic urges. This is the man who could even delight in "renting" a high-class call girl, one who obeys his commands and respects his dominance.

Then there's always the scenario of his meeting up with a successful and well-connected woman, one he feels could serve his needs even better than you. Sounds horrible, doesn't it? But he'd probably have to be quite unhappy in his present marriage to even consider such low behavior. On the other hand, if he realizes he's married to a woman who will ruin him, one way or another, no actions are beneath him.

Overall, though, there's little reason for concern. Chances are you married the Goat who is a pillar of society. And chances are you're a woman of honor and respect. Like most men, he will be tempted. But unlike most men, he values stability and reputation too much to engage in a senseless fling.

REASONS HE MIGHT CHEAT

- If he's on a power trip
- If he meets an attractive woman who could be of great use
- If he's 102 percent sure he could get away with it, with zero consequences
- If he's dying to try out some sexual behavior he finds inappropriate for you

WHAT YOU CAN DO

- Make life so well-structured that he dare not jeopardize it.
- Mention how tragic it is when a great political leader is brought down by a cheap tart.
- Remind him that you admire his integrity and class.
- Pamper him when he's going through a tough period.
- Make sure he's getting enough sex.
- Stay attractive and well-groomed.
- Continue to be a great asset to him and indispensable to his happiness.

SOME THINGS TO TWEAK

One of the best things you could do is get this man to *lighten up*! Sure, we all have just one life to live, but that's even more reason to make it happy, not just "bearable." Fortunately, your Goat will find it a bit easier to enjoy life after forty (when he begins to grow "younger"), but sometimes he's so focused and narrow-minded that he fails to comprehend the need for joy and fun. This is where you have to step in and find ways to add some pleasant diversion to this heavy duty called *life*. That doesn't mean drinking till you get sick or dancing naked on tables—there're plenty of decent ways to amuse oneself. And after bringing some fun into his life, your Goat might learn to be a more positive person.

Another area to work on is your Capricorn man's tendency to judge his happiness by his wealth and social status and by comparing them to others'. First of all, there will always be someone richer or more important. And secondly, why would he think that he would be happier if he was a VIP? Point out the multitude of "important" people who are unhappy, proven by their alcoholism, drugs, and other crutches. Or show him magazine pictures of "powerful" people, the ones who look absolutely miserable and can't even smile. The point is to prove that money and prestige can't buy happiness, and the sooner he learns it, the better. It would be a great idea to read him some philosophy and quote famous proverbs that shed light on the state of happiness. The Goat respects the words of wise men, so he's not likely to ignore them. And think about getting him into meditation. Believe it or not, the goat has *real* spiritual potential buried underneath his ambition—he just has to be made aware of it.

AND HAPPILY EVER AFTER . . .

If you have tons of patience, life with the Goat should become more pleasant as the years pass. It might never be fun or exciting, but what is in the long term? Anyway, "thrilling" marriages (if they even exist) have a quick burnout rate and there's nothing great about that. If you value serenity and security, be assured you've found the right partner. And while the marriages around you are exploding, imploding, or tearing apart at the seams, you'll be relieved to watch yours trudge forward, slowly but surely. You might have to make a bigger time investment in this man than you would in others, but the rewards will be richer and longer-lasting.

Aquarius, the Waterbearer

(about January 21 till about February 19)

After an Aquarius man? Not an easy task if you're looking for a long-term, exclusive relationship. The Aquarius man is an anticonformist at heart, so traditional rules of dating won't fly with him. Any interested girl will have to realize early on that she's dealing with the Waterbearer, put on earth with the lofty task of sustaining humanity with his jug of water. So, obviously, she'll need to interact differently with him than she would with any other man on this planet.

There's a wide range of Aquarius men, from movie-star cool to really weird ones. In any case, there's a distinct quality in him that no other man possesses, a sort of untouchability that intrigues (or irritates) those around him. And because he's not "one of us," he's attracted to odd things (and people) that most of us wouldn't even look at. He even exploits his uniqueness.

The Aquarius facade is aloof and impersonal, which might enrage those femme fatales who can usually count on hypnotizing a man with nothing more than a smoldering stare. Even worse, this guy belongs to everyone, but nobody in particular, and cringes at the mere idea of being possessed by anybody. Yes, he can be enticed by a special girl, but he's the last man to spend sleepless and tormented nights thinking about her. And sex may come a far second to friendship and sympathy in a potential relationship, so don't rely too much on your feminine weapons to seduce him.

In fact, the Aquarius man often has "romantic friendships," or platonic romances . . . however you want to put it. He may eventually want more from a girl he's always known as a friend, or draw out the "friend" aspect from a girl who was initially a one-night stand, but whatever the case, it is clear that the ability to relate as more than lovers is significant to this man. And the ability to share common interests and to exchange intellectual ideas is critical to any potential relationship.

The Aquarius man is a social animal, often belonging to a group, project, or cause. He also needs to spend lots of time with his friends. This can be particularly upsetting for the girl who dreams of spending cozy nights in front of the fireplace watching videos, or for the one who wants a leash around her man's neck. His private life comes after his social life, so most gals will have to make lots of compromises to make it work with him.

Because this guy is totally unpredictable in all domains of life, it's best to expect the unexpected from him, even when it comes to romance. A first date will not necessarily be followed up by a warm phone call or a second date in the following days (in fact, a first or second "date" might not even take place at a romantic restaurant, but at a cocktail party, tennis club, or group meeting). You might not even hear from this guy until the next time you bump into him at the Laundromat or a charity event. This doesn't mean you wore the wrong dress or said the wrong things on your first "date." It simply means this guy has his own timing and standards, and tough luck if they don't conform to yours.

No, he sees no reason to follow any protocol in the dating arena, so he's not the man to have the seduction planned out, as in romance on the first date, kiss on the second date, sex on the third, etc. That's plain boring. This is a guy who thrives on the unknown and the unexpected. And he can disappear from your life without warning, only to pop up again months (or years) later.

Maybe the next time you get together, it will be for a workout at the gym or a trip to the latest electronics store. Romantic? Not really. Confusing? Yes. Sometimes you won't understand if he wants to be your friend or your lover. One day he'll treat you like his sister, the next day like his flame (but one that never burns too hot, for no woman can really inflame his senses and passions). No, this man is not burning with lust for his latest flirt. His approach to the female sex is more intellectual and friendly. And he's not comfortable in emotional situations anyway, so he usually shies away from contact that becomes too intensely intimate.

If there is a kind of girl who can get this guy ticking, it's the glamorous star-type, with a cool appeal and untouchable aura, not the sensual bedroom queen. Glamour is cerebral and airy, and stirs the intellect instead of the "you know what." Glamour is also somewhat eccentric, and anything out of the norm can entice this guy's imagination. Even if you don't

THE AQUARIUS MAN IS

AT BEST	AT WORST
Original	Aloof
Clever	Unreliable
Genius	Eccentric
Curious	Hot and Cold
Friendly	Disinterested
Quirky	Bizarre
Independent	Erratic
Liberal	Unstable
Progressive	Radical
Inventive	Shallow
Sociable	Opportunistic
Unique	Stubborn
Fun	Perverse
Humanitarian	Impractical
Tolerant	Hypocritical

consider yourself this type of girl, you can bring out aspects of her somewhat in your persona. Be friendly but cool, somewhat untouchable. Try to radiate a sort of special aura, one that says, "I'm different" (interpreted as "I'm interesting" to the Water-bearer), when you walk into a party. Play some tricks, exhibit some quirky behavior from time to time, and, most of all, spend lots of time with "the gals" and your own set of people he has no ties to. Don't make rules, makes scenes, or give ultimatums. Be a free spirit and you may just capture (and keep) this guy's attention.

The Aquarius man is great for one-night stands, friendship, and very open relationships. And he's really unique, no doubt about that. You can keep him for the longer term if you are clever enough to stay cool and continue to intrigue his curiousity, but never expect him to declare his absolute, exclusive, and unwavering devotion. There are just too many places to go and people to meet in this world, and this man does not want to miss out. If you can convince him that you share his philosophy, maybe you could form a team over the long term, as long as you never try to possess him. In any case, you will never meet anyone quite like him, and he might teach you a thing or two.

SOME FAMOUS AQUARIUS MEN

John Travolta, James Dean, Robbie Williams, Gene Hackman, Christian Bale, Tom Selleck, Joe Pesci, Robert Altman, John Belushi, Axl Rose, Mikhail Baryshnikov, Ronald Reagan, Franklin D. Roosevelt, Charles Lindbergh, Thomas Edison, Eddie Van Halen, Clark Gable, Paul Newman, Michael Jordan, John McEnroe, Tom Brokaw, Dick Cheney, Placido Domingo, Wolfgang Amadeus Mozart

MUST HAVE BEEN AN AQUARIUS MAN

Superman

THE SEDUCTION

The Aquarius man is always interested in the new and untried, so any newcomer to school or work will initially arouse interest. But to keep the interest going, she'll have to stand out in some way, be it dress, attitude, or allure. An "ordinary" female won't cut it, but neither will a beautiful one if she's boring. This might be the time to showcase some of your quirkier behavior if you've got any, just to catch his eye. If you don't have any, just try to convey an image that's cool or glamorous or even aloof.

If the Aquarius man finds you special enough to want to know, he might approach you like a friend and try to become buddies, or he might integrate himself into your own circle of friends. In any case, he operates spontaneously, so he could ask you out when least expected. And he'll usually maintain a friendly but impersonal facade, just to keep some distance (and to keep you confused).

Again, one never knows how things will evolve with this chap. Each Aquarius man is different. But you'll probably make the best impression if you stay friendly, interesting, and independent—that means having your own agenda and friends. And there's got to be some connection on the intellectual level. Some Aquarius men are really too brilliant to comprehend, so an alert woman should know how to steer him to more manageable topics if he starts talking about the laws of physical science.

When the moment for some bodily interaction arises, forget all the rules and go for it if you feel right about it. This is the guy least likely to look down on a one-night stand (not that this is particularly recommended), because he doesn't care about what's "correct" and what's not. Just don't demand a follow-up phone call or consider yourselves an "item" after your first intimate encounter—it was just a moment of mutual fun, so leave it at that. Let your Aquarius man feel free and act like buddies the next time you see him—he'll appreciate a woman who doesn't confuse sex with love.

SEX

unpredictable, spontaneous, cerebral, different

The Aquarius man is not a hot-blooded animal who lusts after every female body, so naturally, sex is not *that* important to him. Sure, he enjoys sex like most other normal men, but he doesn't *live* for it. And that's probably a good thing. Still, some of the more sensual women might find him a bit aloof in bed, not totally engaged and not totally there. But he is there, at least physically.

Anyway, sex doesn't *have* to consume him. This guy has a way of being able to distance himself emotionally from what's going on under the sheets. If anything, sex with an Aquarius guy should stimulate, satisfy, or simply amuse. And the connection should be at least partly cerebral. That said, this is not the guy who will be overcome by passion and emotional turbulence and take you to new depths of feeling, so don't take sex that seriously and expect something he can't offer.

Obviously, a man like this would get bored of the same routine over and over again, one that requires nothing more than going through the motions. Great sex should stimulate his mind and challenge his previous assumptions. So if you've been wanting to try out some new thing you read about, run it by your Aquarius lover. He's always curious about new ways of doing it. And he's a real trouper. Other men might fantasize about a menage à trois, but this guy would actually try it out. What the heck!

DOS AND DON'TS OF A GREAT RELATIONSHIP

DO

Be glamorous and intriguing.
Be a good friend and listener.
Be fun and exciting.
Be clever and intelligent.
Be able to deal with spontaneity.
Have several hobbies or areas of interest.
Be up-to-date on high-tech gadgets.
Enjoy new people and experiences.
Have a wide and varied circle of friends.
Be open to change.
Make him feel free.
Spend lots of time with your girlfriends or colleagues.
Know how to get along with his friends.
Encourage him in his causes and projects.
Flirt with others (even women!).
Play games (but only clever ones).

DON'T

Be materialistic and greedy.
Be possessive and jealous.
Be rigid and conservative.
Be narrow-minded and provincial.
Be emotional and clingy.
Be too grounded and boring.
Expect long-term planning.
Talk about commitment.
Deprive him of his time with the guys.
Put your relationship before his social life.
Be available every time he rings.
Sit at home and brood when he's out.

Be too predictable.
Make beastly scenes.
Insist that he conform to rules or traditions.
Always be there when he just happens to need you.

BEST WAYS TO IMPRESS

Know how to fly a plane.
Be famous.
Be a candidate for space travel.
Be a trendsetter.
Be the head of some strong and powerful organization.

BEST WAYS TO GET DUMPED

Be a Stepford Wife.
Give him an ultimatum to choose between you and his friends.
Have an emotional breakdown when he says hello to another female.
Start making wedding plans after the first date.
Install a chip in him to monitor his whereabouts via satellite (on the other hand, he could find this novelty quite brilliant).

FASHION

The Aquarius man doesn't worry much about fashion, but he does appreciate a woman with a unique sense of style, one that sets her apart from the others. It all comes down to persona, and there's no doubt that clothes help create one. But it's not just about the clothes—it's about the way one wears them, and the attitude, too. Some girls can throw on anything, even a potato sack, and look really cool (probably because they are really cool in the first place). Still, it also has lots to do with self-confidence and a sense of individuality, so at least there's some hope for the rest of us.

Having said that, though, there's probably no girl who could look cool in Granny's wardrobe, and if there's one man who wouldn't appreciate your grandma's clothes, it's this one (unless, of course, your grandmother happened to be a celebrity). The progressive Aquarius man is more into modern or cutting-edge looks, not petticoats and polyester. He often enjoys the latest trends, as long as a woman is the very first to sport them. Anyway, if you happen to like experimenting, this is the guy to try it on. Just be genius enough to get away with it.

Not surprisingly, the Aquarius man appreciates unique accessories and unusual ways of wearing them, like taking a brooch and making a pendant or a belt decoration out of it, or making a halter top out of a fantastic silk scarf. He also tends to like the more unusual colors, even textures, that other shoppers pass on, so there's always a big selection to choose from when the sales come around. Then there's the gadget-type accessories that drive him mad, like the silver ring that becomes a watch or, better yet, a camera. This curious animal is always on the lookout for the odd, the glamorous, or the next big thing, so impress him with your fashion foresight, if you have any.

GIFT IDEAS: Those that are novel, progressive, and informative

BEER BUDGET

Quirky gadget
Computer software (games)
Zany jokes calendar
Books (futuristic, political, leisure)
Unique tie
Remote-control toy plane

CHAMPAGNE BUDGET
Latest high-tech gizmo
Tickets to a charity event
Film projector and screen
Home satellite system
Glamorous old convertible
Flying lessons

ADD SOME SPICE

A relationship with an Aquarius man will be unpredictable but not necessarily spicy. Still, he's a clever guy and would only appreciate some clever deeds.

Some Ideas

1. Get a unique tattoo on your derriere, and let him figure out if it's real or not.
2. Dare him to make love with you on an airplane.
3. Flirt with a cool stranger to test out his claim of "not being the jealous type."
4. Engage in a brilliant political debate.

IF YOU SENSE A LOOMING BREAKUP

From the very beginning an imminent breakup is always a possibility, so you'll need to stay on high alert at all times. Besides, things with him happen suddenly, so there's usually not enough time to figure out what's going to happen. For that reason, you'd have no time to "sense a looming breakup" —it would usually come out of the blue. So don't make yourself miserable by analyzing his already strange behavior—if it's too late, it's too late.

Danger Signs to Watch For (or predict, if you can see into the future)

- No more sex
- Increasing and obvious boredom on his side
- Drastic changes of plans, even residences, that don't include you
- A sudden, new feminine friendship

If you can actually see future events, and they don't look good, disappear out of his life before he disappears out of yours. If logistics make this impossible, try the buddy breakup. Suddenly and without warning, tell him you're not in the mood for romance and you want to be *friends*. Of course, this bizarre development will rattle him, but he probably won't take you that seriously, so show him you mean business and start dating other men. It would be nice of you to introduce him to potential girlfriends, too, just to make him realize how friendly you actually are. In the meantime, continue to pal around with him, but *don't* let him draw out the lover in you, even after too many drinks. If you intrigue him enough, over a long period of time, he might just invent a clever way to get you back for good.

And if you're really hooked on him, don't despair if he decides to break it off. The Aquarius man is the type who can reappear in your life as unexpectedly as he disappears. This is also the guy capable of breaking up, then getting back together, ten times a year. If you hope for a future reunion, stay on good terms. But that doesn't mean you can't play a few games, too!

AND NEVER FORGET

His essential need for progress and change

HOW MR. AQUARIUS SEES YOU

	AT BEST	AT WORST
Aries	challenging, independent	demanding, exhausting
Taurus	determined, loyal	possessive, dull
Gemini	flirty, popular	dishonest, insecure
Cancer	intuitive, inconstant	traditional, clingy
Leo	confident, creative	arrogant, demanding
Virgo	reasonable, smart	anxious, prudent
Libra	sociable, fair	dependent, snobbish
Scorpio	exciting, daring	intense, controlling
Sagittarius	adventurous, open-minded	simple, unintriguing
Capricorn	loyal, stabilizing	conservative, gloomy
Aquarius	unique, friendly	stubborn, disinterested
Pisces	kind, intriguing	hypersensitive, needy

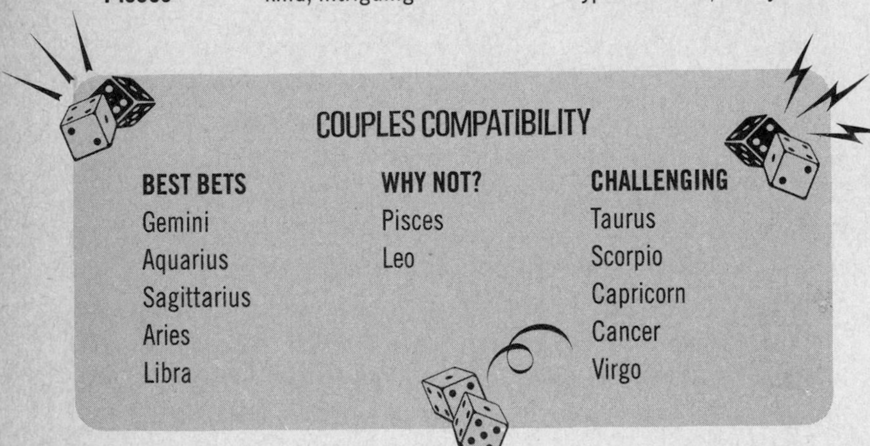

COUPLES COMPATIBILITY

BEST BETS	WHY NOT?	CHALLENGING
Gemini	Pisces	Taurus
Aquarius	Leo	Scorpio
Sagittarius		Capricorn
Aries		Cancer
Libra		Virgo

AQUARIUS MAN (Paul Newman) AND PISCES WOMAN (Joanne Woodward)

This is an interesting couple, to say the least. And they don't have that much in common, except that they're certainly different from the rest of us (which is why they could be good together). The Aquarius man is unique, and it just might be this quality that keeps the complex Pisces woman intrigued in the long run. And this is the guy who will always have something new up his sleeve—a hobby, project, idea—so a relationship with him never gets too boring for Ms. Pisces. In fact, the Aquarius man would be clever to enlist the advice of his Pisces lover, whose sixth sense can intuit what will work and what won't. Still, stubborn Mr. Aquarius wouldn't listen anyway because he knows what he wants and nobody can stop him once he has a plan. What he needs is a buddy, not a guiding light, and someone who enjoys the same activities he does (or at least comprehends them). Ms. Pisces might lose out on the emotional intimacy she so craves in relationships, so it's crucial she has some sort of artistic outlet for her heavy emotional content if she's to stay with the detached Aquarius man. And if she finds it, these unusual people could thrive together in the long run, even though endurance in relationships is neither his nor her specialty. Just proves that everyone has his match.

SOME ADVICE—TAKE IT OR LEAVE IT

YOUR SIGN	
Aries	Do: be enthusiastic about his ideas, projects, and dreams Don't: be egotistical and impose your needs upon his
Taurus	Do: convince him that your different natures may be complementary Don't: try to possess him like an object
Gemini	Do: delight him with your love of novelty and change Don't: disappoint him with your easy lies
Cancer	Do: offer to host great dinner parties for him and his friends Don't: drag him down into your murky, emotional tides

Leo	Do: develop your latent creative abilities and cultivate a unique "style" Don't: be condescending to him or his friends
Virgo	Do: offer your help in any of his ventures Don't: be cynical about his hopes and dreams
Libra	Do: display your people-pleasing skills and social know-how Don't: become totally dependent on him for your happiness
Scorpio	Do: realize you don't "own" him, and never will Don't: scare him away with your intense and suspicious nature
Sagittarius	Do: delight him with your love of adventure and new horizons Don't: be too simple and straightforward
Capricorn	Do: display your patience and trust when he needs his space Don't: be so rigid and intolerant
Aquarius	Do: give each other turns at being "right" Don't: refuse to listen to his advice
Pisces	Do: endear yourself to him with your generosity and compassion Don't: drown him in your emotional waters

Looking Farther Down the Road

TRUE LOVE

THE ENGAGEMENT

Mr. Aquarius has his own rules (or non-rules), so you just never know if he'll ever marry. In fact, this is the dude who thrives in open relationships, with no commitment or expectations, so you could spend years together without any kind of formality. Then, after a singularly great evening, when you're sure he's going to pop the question, he can stun you with "Let's just be friends" or "Guess what, I'm moving to L.A." New developments can happen that fast, when least expected.

Still, your Aquarius man is naturally curious and may just want to learn what this marriage thing is all about, so a proposal is not totally out of the question. Who knows, this unpredictable man could throw you a zinger by proposing after three weeks. But more likely, he'll wait and wait as long as he can, and in the meantime, break up, get back together, leave the country, come back, become friends, become romantic, need "space," etc.

If your Aquarius man at least refers to marriage (positively), he might be toying with the idea, but if he shrinks away from the topic, throw *him* a zinger by announcing that you'll be eloping with a unique and brilliant man next week. If he's really fond of you, he might just suggest ditching the other guy and eloping with him that evening.

If you don't like playing games, you can always try another approach. Look at marriage in a more experimental light, rather than an emotional or formal one. Make it sound novel, or like something cool to do. Stir his curiosity and intrigue him. Just *never* apply pressure, and always let him feel like it was his brilliant idea in the first place.

THE WEDDING

If you've actually managed to get a promise from this man, start making plans before he changes his mind. But whatever happens, don't become all desperate or panicky. Keep up the friendly feeling and stay emotionally detached from the whole wedding affair. Treat it more like an interesting project than a legal and binding event. And in the case that your Aquarius man suggests you elope or head for Vegas on the spur of the moment, you should seriously consider taking him up on his offer.

If you both have the time for planning, though, ask his helpful advice, since he'll definitely have strong opinions. He might want an original wedding, so have a great time brainstorming together. And don't bum him out by mocking some of his weirder ideas, like marrying on a ski slope or in an airplane with some friends. Stay open-minded and keep the preparations interesting. Just be careful the wedding doesn't stay in planning mode forever.

THE HONEYMOON

The Aquarius man would go to the moon if he could, but since it's not yet an option, he has no choice but to settle for an earthly destination. Wherever you decide to go, make sure there are a lot of interesting things to do. This is not the man to drag off to a deserted island with only sex on your mind. Your Aquarius man needs mental stimulation and time to explore. Don't stay in one spot too long, and combine several destinations if you want a longer trip.

And now that you're legally married, don't spoil the trip by acting like a "wife." This should be a buddy vacation, full of laughs, surprises, and great stories—and lots of *space.* Never sulk when your Aquarius man needs his own time. And keep him wondering about your own interesting schemes. It wouldn't hurt, either, to bring along some great books and board games for when you feel like staying in.

MAKING IT IN THE LONG HAUL

If your Aquarius husband likes this thing called marriage after all, he might be happy he made the ingenuous decision to couple up and look forward to many interesting years together. But if it's more the case of "Been there, done that," your days together could be numbered. The first couple of years (or even months) will be crucial in determining if he can handle this institution, so make your best effort during the newlywed period. That means making him feel free, giving lots of space, and never truly "settling." Friendship will matter most, and the ability to applaud his hopes and projects.

DOS AND DON'TS FOR LASTING BLISS

DO

Give him the freedom he needs.
Keep your door open (at all hours) for his friends.
Be flexible to sudden change.
Stay optimistic and pleasant.
Experiment with different hobbies.
Allow him to express his (sometimes radical) views.
Keep your cool during disputes.
Bedazzle him with your great ideas.
Maintain an active social life.
Continue to spend lots of time with your own set of friends.
Stay open-minded and tolerant.
Be ready for adventure.
Keep the lines of communication open.
Write him clever e-mails.
Stay independent and self-sufficient.
Surprise him with unique gifts or spontaneous plans.

DON'T

Treat him differently now that you're "legal."
Snub any of his quirky friends.
Always dwell on the past.
Scold him for his flakiness.
Become an emotional wreck.

Insist that you do everything together.
Take away his right to privacy.
Freak out when he forgets to come home.
Try to possess him (mentally, emotionally, or physically).
Bribe or manipulate him.
Become dark and menacing.
Create friction among your mutual friends.
Always count on him.
Expect passionate love overtures.
Flinch when he flirts with other gals.

EARTHLY BLISS (AKA SEX)

Nothing about sex with this man will be "earthly," because he's detached from his carnal side. And yet as the years go by, this eternally curious guy may become more and more interested in experimenting with different approaches and positions. He may even want to explore the repertory of the *Kama Sutra*. Still, don't expect sex to become steamy and hot, because this guy just doesn't understand the meaning of fervent passion. Even a delicious love nest or sexy getup can't coax him into wasting hours in decadent fleshly pleasures. The Aquarius man has things to see and do, and no vamp will hold him back from his friends and activities.

To keep things interesting, the Aquarius man might use his inventive genius and oddball timing to make the most out of any experience. He may even want to try out some high-tech toys or other sexual paraphernalia to get some new kicks. Just keep him stimulated, be a good sport, and don't pout if you can never elicit the rapture you dream of.

And don't sulk if he seems to be losing interest in sex, either. There will be periods when he might not touch you, not because he doesn't love you, but because he's in a different groove. Then, just when you think you've lost him forever, he could dazzle you with new urgency and frequency. A specialist in comebacks, this kid will reemerge when least expected.

AND CHEATING . . . ?

Sure, you may expect the unexpected, at any time in your marriage, so nothing's out, even a little "cheating." (But he *hates* that word, which implies breaking some sort of law—he'd much rather think of it as "tinkering.") Still, you don't have to worry about your Aquarius man going out on the prowl. Things just kind of come to him spontaneously, and his reactions depend on his mind-set at the moment.

Being the way he is, a one-night stand is not out of the question, but it probably wouldn't be the beginning of a secret and lasting love affair that you'd never find out about. More likely, it would happen out of the blue, and have little effect on his feelings for you. Then, another likely scenario would be the romanticizing of a girl who was always a friend. Again, it would probably lead more to a short-term diversion—in this case, fun kisses and togetherness—than a full-blown liaison. Anyway, the Aquarius man is pretty honest, so he'd probably admit a fling if you really had to know.

Sometimes an Aquarius man "tinkers" just to reassure himself of his independence. He hates to think he's "owned" by anyone, including you, so hooking up with other gals is often "proof" of his freedom. Still, this man can be loyal. And he hates to cause pain. If he's really thinking long-term with you, he should stay true. Besides, he's ruled by his head, not by his you-know-what, so he has more self-control than some other beasts out there. On the other hand, he could suddenly leave you, just like that, to regain total freedom in all areas of his life. You just never know with this one.

REASONS HE MIGHT CHEAT

- If it's just the right moment
- If you make him feel imprisoned and restricted
- If his curiosity is killing him
- If there're no strings attached
- If he meets a truly unique woman

WHAT YOU CAN DO

- Refuse to obsess about it.
- Stay open-minded to new and daring sexual experiences.
- Tell him you admire his loyalty and control.
- Change your look and attitude so he can experience "different" women.
- Become buddies with his friends so you're not too excluded.
- Tell him he can talk to you about *anything*.
- Be the best friend he dare not lose.

SOME THINGS TO TWEAK

How do you help a guy who has his own set of rules? It won't be easy, or maybe even possible, but you could at least try explaining the benefits of compromise. The first thing you may want to make him aware of is his erratic timing and sudden reorientations. Sympathize with his love of spontaneity, but let him know that it's hard on others (not you, but everyone around him). Compliment him on being light-years ahead of the rest of us mortals, but explain how he might experience more meaningful relationships and worldly success if he could somehow coordinate his time with ours. Forgetting or postponing meetings and making sudden and drastic shifts in plans is okay from time to time, but eventually he'll be branded as a big *flake* if he can't be a little more dependable and stable. And that's when some people will simply give up on him. Try appealing to his sense of fairness when stressing that his random (even selfish) timing makes things difficult for others.

Then you'd do him a big favor by drawing out his more sensual side, just to make him more "touchable." Get him in contact with the earth—dirt, sand, plants, trees. Plan a project you can enjoy together, like trampling on grapes in a vineyard or building a treehouse from natural materials. Have a food fight, throw a pie in his face. Challenge him to a round of wrestling in the mud. Just beckon this man back to basics and remind him that we just came out of the wilderness yesterday. Sure, we've come a long way, thanks to people like him, but that doesn't mean we have nothing to gain from our more "primitive" nature.

AND HAPPILY EVER AFTER . . .

Life with an Aquarius man will be full of happy moments, but they can come as quickly as they go. As for "ever after," that's something he can't commit to today. But why stress out over things so far in the future? We could be invaded by aliens in thirty years, or something worse. And you'd be lucky to know this progressive man, who plans for such events, anyway. So don't brood over a golden anniversary you may never have—you'll see and do more things in five years with this man than you would spending forty years with another. And who knows, you may just surprise everyone (including yourself) by ending up the most enduring couple of all—anything is possible with this man. Still, the best advice is to appreciate the moment and live each day to the fullest—what's here today won't necessarily be here tomorrow.

Pisces, the Fish

(about February 20 till about March 20)

Fascinated by a Pisces man? Then be warned that you're dealing with the most complex man of all! And the most intuitive. He can size you up in two seconds and tell you the things he knows you want to hear, so be wary of words that are too good to be true. Yes, he can be a charmer if he wants, but endurance is not his specialty, so catching this Fish for the long term is harder than you think (though he can be tempted by many a bait!).

Getting to know a Pisces man is an accomplishment in itself, because he's the most enigmatic of creatures, with a rich inner life most of us don't understand or are even aware of. Fantasy, dreams, and a great imagination are all part of his private world, which he often prefers to the real world out there. This is why he has been accused of being a dreamer or a flake. When the going gets tough, he can retreat to his imaginary universe, where everything is nice and pretty (and sometimes his vehicles of escape are books, cinema, vacations, and, worse, drugs and alcohol).

But there's something good coming from this. His notion of imagination and fiction enable him to carry out the most magical relationships. In fact, anything romantic or enchanting attracts him, and it's in such a climate that he thrives. Here's the guy who will delight in a late-night meeting in the park or a secret getaway to an exotic island. And it's for precisely this reason that he can be tempted to sneak off with another gal behind your back! The whole concept of "forbidden fruit" (or in his case, forbidden bait) is *so* intriguing to the Pisces man. This is why he often functions better as the secret lover than the official husband.

The Fish is slippery in love, not because he's necessarily tricky, but because he's in love with romance. And we all know that romance is hard to maintain over the long term. The real problem arises the day his rose-colored glasses fall off and he's forced to regard his girlfriend in the harsh light of the here and now. Yesterday his girl was dancing under the soft light of the moon, and today she's struggling with telephone bills and broken nails. Is there anything less romantic? Not in the eyes of a Fish. He wants the drama and romance to continue, and the girl who wants him will have the almost impossible job of trying to maintain a magical relationship in an unmagical world. Maybe this is why the Fish has the habit of swimming away when a relationship becomes too "real," in search of romance elsewhere.

The Pisces man is especially empathetic, so he's often attracted to females who have their own set of problems. Or who are in complex situations. Or who are legally out of his bounds (e.g., married). Or who make him suffer somehow. (He must find something glamorous about suffering, because he seems to seek it subconsciously.) And a female who can lure him into a web of fantasy, intrigue, and romance can really keep him hooked. The Fish finds nothing tasty about simplicity, and may swim from woman to woman until he finds the one who has permanent allure.

The other kind of Fish might choose the goldfish scenario, content to be cared for and fed in a golden aquarium. This is the type who seeks a strong female, and it wouldn't hurt if she had some money, too. (He could even become somewhat of a leech.) But if he's lucky, this solid woman would have the energy and patience necessary to help him exploit his amazing talents. And then she'd have a happy, even successful, Fish.

The Pisces man has great potential, but a relationship with him is often cloudy. Difficulties may arise when you catch him in a magnificent lie, one that defies all logic. It's not really his fault, though, because he sometimes gives in to his active imagination and ends up telling people things as he'd like them to be, or as he believes them to be. Just be wary when you smell something fishy, and try to draw the truth out of him in a gentle way.

Whatever you do, though, make sure you can tell the difference between fact and fiction. Because of his need for color and melodrama, the themes of illusion, deception, and betrayal usually play a paramount role in the Pisces man's life, be it in business or love. Will he be the victim or the perpetrator? It depends. Just make sure *you* aren't the dupe of one of his grand fabrications or shocking infidelities, and use your own intuition to figure out early on if a relationship with this guy is for real or not.

THE PISCES MAN IS

AT BEST	AT WORST
Charming	Dishonest
Idealistic	Passive
Romantic	Naive
Intuitive	Unstable
Sensitive	Irrational
Charismatic	Confused
Sacrificing	Messy
Compassionate	Irresponsible
Generous	Suffering
Artistic	Complex
Creative	Indulgent
Caring	Lazy
Emotional	Escapist
Spiritual	Unrealistic
Musical	Self-Deluded

This is a special guy, indeed, and the best bet for a gal like you to keep him on the line is to enshroud yourself in a cloud of mystery and always keep him wondering and guessing. He is intuitive, yes, but don't let him figure you out completely, not now and not ever. Keep your relationship complex and magical, and indulge him in his need for romance so he doesn't go looking for it elsewhere.

SOME FAMOUS PISCES MEN

Bruce Willis, Billy Crystal, Jon Bon Jovi, Alan Greenspan, Rob Lowe, Michael Eisner, Prince Albert of Monaco, Rupert Murdoch, Edgar Cayce, Michael Dell, Mikhail Gorbachev, Steve Jobs, Joe Lieberman, Kurt Cobain, Andy Gibb, Bugsy Siegel, George Harrison, Ted Kennedy, Fats Domino, Peter Fonda, Dr. Seuss, Nat King Cole, Ron Howard, Victor Hugo, Sandro Botticelli, Ariel Sharon, Michael Caine

MUST HAVE BEEN A PISCES MAN

Romeo *(Romeo and Juliet)*

THE SEDUCTION

The Fish will notice any fascinating woman, but he's not at his best in day-to-day situations—he'd be much more receptive to your vibes in an extraordinary or exceptional setting, like at a costume party or during a trip on a tropical island. But even if you see him at work every day, you can still tempt him with some mysterious or glamorous behavior. And once he notices you, he'll be hooked until he gets to know you better.

The Pisces man might spend more time fantasizing about you than planning a strategy to ask you out, though, because he's not especially aggressive. Besides, he loves to dream, and this way he can always have the ending he wants. Still, if your charms have really worked on him, he should come around eventually. And if he's had a few drinks, he can become very bold in approaching you.

The Fish is too disorganized to follow a well-planned dating strategy, so even when you begin dating, it's often irregular or last-minute. For him, the best night begins with a few drinks and then . . . who knows? It could end in a gourmet restaurant, a drive-in, a secluded beach, or a steamy Jacuzzi. The more fabulous, the better. The Fish thrives in ambiguous situations, where the element of the unknown lingers deliciously in the air, so don't cool him off by demanding an hour-to-hour agenda. Try surrendering to the moment and letting the tides take you where they may.

Just make sure he's not married before you start an adventure. And be wary of the "I'm separated" or "I'm getting divorced" claim. When you know he's for real, let him seduce you in a climate of romance or drama, like a midnight rendezvous in a swimming pool or in a sumptuous hotel room. And maintain an immortal mystique so he spends sleepless nights thinking about you.

SEX

magical, tender, spiritual, emotional

Sex is no simple affair to the Pisces man. How could it be for someone as complex as him? This first-rate dreamer may even be more enchanted by the romance leading up to sex than the act itself. In any case, sex should be more inspiring than the textbook kind.

Mood and atmosphere will always play a big role in good sex for the Pisces man. This is the guy who'd like to experience all the feelings and emotions one can only read about in a novel, so it's no surprise that's he's disappointed more often than not. Still, after years of experience, he might become more realistic about his expectations and satisfied with sex of more "normal" proportions.

But if fictional sex is impossible, maybe something near divine sex is not. And divine sex suggests something marvelous, spiritual, mysterious, lovely, even transcendent. Through sex, he might escape himself, or escape the world, hoping to find a lost paradise. And the best thing you can do is give in to his altered state and let him fuse into your tender, loving self.

DOS AND DON'TS OF A GREAT RELATIONSHIP

DO

Do your best to keep him intrigued.
Be strong when necessary.
Enjoy romance and games.
Maintain a secret side to yourself.
Add some magic to everyday life.
Let him in on some of your sorrows.
Lend a shoulder to cry on.
Support him during his low moments.
Enjoy music and cinema.
Hide your flaws.
Let him dream.
Support his gut instincts.
Be musical, if possible.
Respect the poor and underprivileged.
Get yourself into complex situations.

DON'T

Be cold and ruthless.
Be unimaginative and boring.
Be hard and cynical.
Be too intellectual and abstract.
Invade his private space.
Disappoint him by not living up to his ideals.
Get too caught up in the more mundane details of life.
Mock his ideals and dreams.
Demand reason at all times.
Press for commitment.
Hurt his feelings.
Leave him alone for too long.
Encourage him to escape reality.
Take advantage of his goodness.
Burden him with huge responsibilities.

BEST WAYS TO IMPRESS

Live on a magnificent yacht.
Have the biggest wine cellar in town.
Be tied into the film world somehow.
Have a dream/fantasy lifestyle worthy of the movies.

BEST WAYS TO GET DUMPED

Give him a nine P.M. curfew.
See life like reality TV (versus a colorful saga).
Have a "no drinking" policy in your house.
Be unable to swim.
Betray his idea of what a woman should be.

FASHION

The Fish is not the most worldly man around, so he's usually unaware of the latest fashion trends, but he does love clothes, especially for their ability to create a certain aura. In fact, a particularly sublime outfit could make such an impression on him that he could be immediately captivated by the unknown woman who wears it. So clothes don't have to be expensive or very up to date, but they should be effective.

All Fish love very feminine clothes, especially those that combine a little mystery, romance, or glamour. And any "magical" cuts and fabrics would send him to cloud nine. But he also loves a female who can mutate from one look to another, like an actress who changes her wardrobe for different films (unless it's a Western). Sometimes the Pisces man sees life as through a camera lens, so he appreciates costumes and dressing up more than others. Anyway, he needs fantasy, so the no-makeup/sweatsuit look will only disappoint him.

Sure enough, the right accessories can only enhance the ideal look. And because of his innate creative streak, he'd really admire some of the more artistic or romantic touches. Shimmer, frills and trills, gauzy or fluid cover-ups and other special extras can only help create a look worthy of the silver screen. As for colors, all shades of the sea fascinate him—every possible hue of green, blue, and silver sends shivers down his spine. (Too much black and gray depresses him.) And this guy has a thing about feet, so a perfect pedicure and fantastic open-toed heels would really do the trick.

GIFT IDEAS: Those that are romantic, fantastic, philanthropic, or serve as a means of (benign) escape

BEER BUDGET

DVD of an epic film
Homeless dog
Cologne
Best-selling novel
Beachwear
Music CDs

CHAMPAGNE BUDGET

Top-of-the-line aquarium
Sophisticated DVD and stereo sound system
Donation to his favorite charity
Video camera
Sailboat
Surprise weekend getaway

ADD SOME SPICE

You can never add too much spice to this relationship, but you might have trouble thinking up new ways to entice him.

Some Ideas

1. After a romantic date, get into a melodramatic fight, make a grandiose escape, then let him capture you and make up with climactic love.
2. Meet him at midnight on a secluded beach, then drink champagne and make love.
3. Write, shoot, and act out a romantic movie together.
4. Disappear for a couple days and let him suffer your mysterious absence.

IF YOU SENSE A LOOMING BREAKUP

The disenchanted Fish won't hang around for long. And he's not the type to sit you down and have an honest talk about a poor relationship—if anything, he'll lie or escape or disappear out of your life (and maybe reappear when he feels like seeing you again). Still, he's pretty fluid, so you may be able to change his mind if you can spot trouble early enough.

Danger Signs to Watch For

- More secret or mysterious behavior
- Increasing dishonesty
- More drinking and carousing
- Greater need for escape while in your company

This is the man with a sympathetic ear, so talk to him if you're worried about your relationship. Just never use cold, hard logic to try to get to him—he's especially sensitive to melodrama, so open your heart and keep the emotion level high. Of course, he'd rather lie than hurt you, so he may resort to some fabrication, just to appease you. Still, you should get him to tell you what's bothering him, because it could be something easy to change.

If you're better at playing games, though, this is the man to challenge. Maybe the best way to touch him is with fanciful behavior, straight out of a movie. Throw in some new developments and subplots that make your life that much richer (e.g., a long-lost love coming into town). Or intrigue him with the notion that he never really knew you in the first place, and let him suffer with the realization that he might lose you somehow. Strike him in the gut, where it really hurts, and get him to rethink his devotion.

If nothing seems to work and he still wants to end it, then give him a good-bye he'll never forget. Appeal to drama and emotions, even if that means slapping him in the face. It's better to go out with a big bang than a weak fizzle, especially if you hope to hook up with him in the future. The Fish has no memory for crisp, polite words, but he never forgets dramatic visuals and the emotions they stir up, so leave him with a memorable souvenir he can cherish in his dreams.

AND NEVER FORGET

His essential need to dream

HOW MR. PISCES SEES YOU

	AT BEST	AT WORST
Aries	stimulating, passionate	selfish, straightforward
Taurus	affectionate, artistic	pragmatic, unspiritual
Gemini	versatile, cheerful	logical, unfeeling
Cancer	emotional, nurturing	crabby, vengeful
Leo	creative, strong	domineering, arrogant
Virgo	stabilizing, helpful	rational, unimaginative
Libra	diplomatic, accommodating	shallow, snobbish
Scorpio	intense, mysterious	vindictive, biting
Sagittarius	spiritual, adventurous	unreliable, tactless
Capricorn	dependable, sincere	cold, realistic
Aquarius	humane, visionary	aloof, cerebral
Pisces	romantic, sensitive	negligent, weak

COUPLES COMPATIBILITY

BEST BETS	WHY NOT?	CHALLENGING
Scorpio	Aries	Virgo
Cancer	Taurus	Capricorn
Leo	Sagittarius	Pisces
Aquarius	Libra	Gemini

PISCES MAN (Prince Andrew) and LIBRA WOMAN (Fergie)

These signs have a bit in common, at least enough for the short term (and maybe even longer). People born under both signs enjoy beauty and harmony, and they're usually gentle and kind. And the Libra woman has no problem staying at the superficial level, where everything is nice and pleasant. But the Pisces man needs something more eventually—like drama and emotion and lots of romance. Unfortunately, some Libra women have insatiable appetites for luxury and society and end up neglecting the emotional needs of their husbands. What happens eventually is the disillusioned Pisces man retreats into his private world and suffers in silence or, on the other hand, swims away in search of a more ideal love. And if the Pisces man goes into retreat, his Libra woman can easily fall into the trap of another man, the kind who can flatter her and make her feel *attractive* again. The funny thing is that infidelity can both disappoint and intrigue the Pisces man. He might swim away for now, but you can bet this fluid creature secretly harbors a fascination for the woman who was able to make him suffer.

SOME ADVICE—TAKE IT OR LEAVE IT

YOUR SIGN	
Aries	DO: help motivate him to exploit his talents DON'T: hurt his feelings with your direct insults
Taurus	DO: share your mutual love of the good life DON'T: stick your pragmatism down his throat
Gemini	DO: indulge in your love of complex situations DON'T: ask him too many questions and drown him in trivial chatter
Cancer	DO: endear yourself to him with your emotional tenderness DON'T: let one of his bad moods upset you
Leo	DO: delight him with your innate creative streak DON'T: pretend you are perfect and have no problems
Virgo	DO: give him a healthy dose of realism from time to time DON'T: bother him with the minutiae of daily life
Libra	DO: showcase your sense of aesthetics and justice DON'T: disappoint him with your difficulty to see beyond the surface
Scorpio	DO: impress him with your emotional strength DON'T: use and abuse him
Sagittarius	DO: cultivate your innate spiritual side DON'T: be totally devoid of mystery
Capricorn	DO: be the sturdy rock he can depend on DON'T: deny him your emotions and heart
Aquarius	DO: intrigue him with your originality DON'T: be too airy and untouchable
Pisces	DO: share your mutual love of romance DON'T: lapse into escapism together

Looking Farther Down the Road

TRUE LOVE

THE ENGAGEMENT

Catching this Fish for keeps won't be easy, unless he's fallen for your particularly extraordinary bait. Otherwise, you might sit and wait, wondering where the tides will carry you. The tricky thing about this Fish is his ability to escape just when things are getting serious or binding. Or he could just stay elusive, not wanting to leave you yet not rushing to officially hook up. And the more you try to snag him, the more fugitive he becomes.

The trick is to make him believe he'll miss out on the best opportunity of his life if he lets *you* get away. Gentle persuasion and subtle gestures might be enough to enlighten some Fish, but others need more theatrics to stir them to action—romance, tears, suffering, mystery, intrigue, even taboos. Still, don't let him keep your hopes up forever with vague and illusory "promises." This is the cad who could keep you hanging in there for years, just to disappear one night and elope with your best friend! So use your intuition to figure him out early on.

THE WEDDING

Now that it's official, don't make the mistake of setting the wedding date in the far future—the longer you wait, the more excuses your Fish can find to get off the hook. Keep the planning period short and efficient, but also vague and mysterious. And don't take all the magic out of it by burdening him with duties, accounts, and responsibilities. You want to keep him guessing and marveling as the big day (night) approaches instead of looking for the easiest exit.

The biggest factor that will play into a successful party is the climate or atmosphere. This event should stir up his most profound feelings and really seem special. A nighttime wedding, with its starry sky and tinge of mystery, could do much to impress this man. And *water,* in all its forms—oceans, lakes, streams, pools, ponds, fountains, falls—could only add an otherworldly touch. Use your imagination to think of other props that could enhance the atmosphere, such as candles, lily pads, cabanas, tents, hidden nooks and make-out spots, beautiful music, romantic decorations, delicate flowers, and enough of his favorite elixir to go around. This wedding should enchant and bring out the romantic fool in him.

THE HONEYMOON

If there's one man who lives for vacations, it's this one. Your Pisces husband will be delighted to escape the hectic world and lose time together for a few hedonistic, lazy, and romantic weeks (months, if he could get away with it!), so don't insist on six A.M. wake-up calls and loaded agendas. Splurge on room service, cocktails, and pampering, and have your DO NOT DISTURB sign handy. Lounge around with him guiltlessly, share some champagne on a secluded beach under the stars, discover some enticing night locales, and indulge in secret pleasures.

Just don't ruin his dream with bills, timetables, and unfinished business—for once, your Fish would love to experience a life of no responsibility. And keep the atmosphere intriguing. This is not the time to lay down your house rules, or explain why you wax, rather than shave, your armpits. If anything, you should bedazzle him with fantastic and impractical behavior one only reads about in novels. Seize the moment and just go for it—you have the rest of your life to be rational.

Honeymoon Sex

The last thing you would want to do is disappoint your impressionable husband, so make sure your first intimate post-wedding encounter takes him to new heights of bliss. Of course, that means planning a seduction worthy of a romantic novel—dim the lights, have the chilled champagne ready, and emerge from nowhere as a silk-clad siren, tempting him to do the unthinkable. Or add some mystery by arranging a secret meeting in a dark enclosure under the light of the moon. Caress him with your heavenly kisses, inspire him with your beguiling smile, and dare him to go where no man has gone before.

MAKING IT IN THE LONG HAUL

The years to come will be no picnic. Unless you're an unbelievably strong, patient, and intuitive woman, your Pisces husband's actions (or non-actions) could send you over the edge. But, on the flip side, there will always be a "new development," so things stay rather interesting. The Fish loves complex situations, so successful married life should play out like an epic film, full of subplots, turning points, reversals, anticlimaxes, and climaxes. At the same time, you'll have to take on the bigger workload and deal with most of the marriage maintenance (while keeping up your mystique, sense of humor, and sanity). Your Fish is blessed with some of the rarest assets known to mankind, and in the hands of the right woman, he can be molded into an exceptional human being, and an exceptional husband. So get some rest—you have lots of work to do!

DOS AND DON'TS FOR LASTING BLISS

DO

Cultivate a romantic atmosphere in everyday life (so he doesn't go looking for trouble).
Encourage him to talk about his problems.
Help him find healthy ways to "escape" (e.g., arts, books, sports).
Invest in a state-of-the-art home entertainment center.
Leave the door open for his stray friends.
Take part in some philanthropic activities together.
Feed his soul with music.
Encourage him to be honest with you and others.
Take care of the household finances.
Dress up from morning till evening.
Have separate bathrooms.
Strive to make sense of his unrelenting dreams and visions.
Seek help for him early if problems develop.
Show him you care about his well-being.
Home in on his hidden talents and help him exploit them.
Plan plenty of vacation and leisure time.

DON'T

Be too predictable and straightforward.
Grow cold and indifferent.
See everything in black and white.
Be too gullible or let him take you for a ride.
Imprison him in a boring and routine life.
Let him figure you out completely.
Make him believe you haven't the capacity to understand him.
Leave him alone for too long.
Let others take advantage of his goodness.
Make him feel unwanted or unloved.

Insist on all work and no play.
Insist on rationale and logic all the time.
Let him believe he was meant to suffer.
Let him pull you down into the abyss.
Give up on him (just yet).

EARTHLY BLISS (AKA SEX)

Make that "heavenly" bliss. There's nothing earthly about the Pisces man's sexual ideal—if anything, it's ethereal and probably impossible for you to fully comprehend. Still, sex is sex, so the physical motions are the same, but what goes on in his head while you're under the sheets is an otherworldly matter.

As the years go by, your Fish might need more and more fantasy to enrich sexual experience, so encourage him to let you in on his secret fantasies, and be open to playing them out. Variety and surprise play into the picture, too. Your bedroom is not the only place in the world to make love—use your imagination to discover new places and scenarios, the more complicated the better. Just never let sex become routine or boring—you'll have to create magic each time if you want to keep this Fish hooked for life.

Then there's also the Pisces man who lives for melodrama, so we're talking passionate, forbidden, or tormenting sex. If you grow weary of thinking up new schemes to entice him, read lots of trashy novels for inspiration. And never underestimate the power of cinema. To get the juices flowing, immerse yourselves in torrid cinematic love scenes, then take the passion back to the bedroom and unleash it on each other. Let him play out his fantasies with you so he doesn't replace you with another actress.

AND CHEATING . . . ?

At the very least, your Pisces man will eventually "meander" in his dreams. And if you're unable to infuse your marriage with the emotional drama he craves, he's likely to find it in illicit affairs and romances. Plus, there's something *so* intriguing about forbidden sex and impossible loves, more so than anything he can find in a "legal" relationship. Anyway, there's a good chance you wouldn't even know, because this man operates well in secrecy. At the same time, though, he tends to be messy and irresponsible, so sooner or later you might sniff him out. And the funny thing is that if you confront him, even with outstanding evidence, he could look you straight in the eye and totally deny any wrongdoing (and even believe it in his own little mind).

Be assured, though, he would never intentionally set out to hurt you. And it's *hard* being him. You can't imagine what it's like to deal with an overactive state of confusion, dreams, and delusions, so maybe you should lay off and have pity. If you believe in any sort of higher love, and if you have the goodness in your heart to sympathize, understand, and forgive, you should be able to survive his rather harmless infidelities.

Just don't accept any indiscreet carousing and womanizing. If he ever gets to the point where he shows little or no respect for fundamental loyalty and honesty, let him off the hook and send him downstream. But if you're in love with the kinder, romantic Fish, do everything in your power to keep your relationship passionate, mysterious, and fulfilling so he's not too tempted to look elsewhere.

REASONS HE MIGHT CHEAT

- If he craves fresh romance
- If he's sure you won't find out
- If he can't deny a mystical attraction
- If he's far from home
- If you kill his romantic dream

WHAT YOU CAN DO

- Play along with his fantasies.
- Tell him it's okay to *dream* about it.
- Seduce him in forbidden places and circumstances.
- Sprinkle your lives with magic and romance.
- Let him know how much his infidelity would hurt you.
- Tell him the "others" would use him up, then throw him away.
- Get him to grow so passionate about a hobby that he forgets his silly fantasies.

SOME THINGS TO TWEAK

You've got a lot of material to work with here. So where to begin? Maybe at the feet, which enable him to take the next escape route. In time you'll notice that the Pisces man prefers to run from problems rather than confront them. Of course, his feet don't provide the only means of escape. Dreams, books, vacations, lies, alcohol, and drugs can do very well, too. Maybe one of the best ways to persuade him to rise to a challenge is to serve as a fighting model yourself. Or impress him by getting him to read the memoirs of a strong man he idolizes. Don't let him believe he can't change, because he's the most adaptable man out there. Support him, encourage him, and applaud his more daring feats, however small they are. A few small successes could lead to a big achievement, and a changed man.

Then it would be big of you to help him create some structure in his physical and emotional life so he would have the necessary foundation to do something great with his life. Sure, he might rather live a passive existence, just going with the flow and bumping into a few logs here and there. But that just won't do. You have to make him realize he was given way too much potential and talent (more than the rest of us) to let it go to waste, and that a lot of other people could really benefit from his masterpieces, be they in art, medicine, science, music, or economics. Putting it in such grandiose terms might impress the Fish and give him more desire to achieve.

A complex man like this will always find it difficult to relate in a world among us simpletons, so encourage your Fish to operate on a more basic level and leave his intricacies for his daydreams. After filtering out all the superfluous stuff, he'll be left with a divine and tender heart, one that can add lots of joy to the lives of those around him.

AND HAPPILY EVER AFTER . . .

Happy endings don't only occur in Hollywood. Even life with a Pisces man could leave you smiling. Still, there'll be all the obstacles to success you could expect in any intricate movie. And lots of tears and sorrows. But if you know how to direct your life together, you could live out a marriage worthy of an Academy Award. So get your act together now and create a love story that others can only dream about. Who said real life can't be better than the movies?

Appendix
Some Unusual Forms of Sun Signs

ARIES

The Master-of-the-Universe: This is the Aries man who really thinks the world revolves around him (to the extreme). It can get to the point where he thinks any behavior and conduct is permitted. He has few friends and a lot of enemies, but he can be irresistibly attractive.

The Warrior: This is the Aries man who's always angry or always wants to fight. Everyone is a potential enemy, he even has fights with people over parking spaces. He probably has a chip on his shoulder and it's probably not a good idea to date him until he's had some counseling in anger management.

The Primate: You'd think this guy just came out of the jungle. Totally uncivilized, he has zero regard for others and can be something of a brute. Very unattractive, but quite rare, too.

TAURUS

The Playboy (or Gigolo): The Taurus man who just doesn't want to work—he'd rather enjoy the highlife, compliments of a trust fund or rich friends. If he has no money, he can turn into the Gigolo-type instead, taking a free ride off rich women.

The Super-Rich Bull: Self-made or rich at birth, this type of bull has a voracious appetite for women, sex, luxury, and all that money can buy. He likes to think there's a price for everything and is convinced an emerald and diamond necklace can secure him any female he wants.

The Granola: Not everyone's cup of tea, but he might please some other nature nuts out there. This Taurus guy is always outdoors, for work or leisure or both. Unlike some other Bulls, he could care less about money—he's high enough on all the fresh air. (But, he might not be a regular bather.)

The Bulldozer: This is a rare bull, hopefully nearing extinction. His greed is so immense, he'll roll over anyone and anything in his unreasonable quest for power, money or land. Stay far away from this one!

GEMINI

The Bore: For some obscure reason, there's a Gemini man out there who's the biggest dud in the world. He's incredibly boring, and sounds like a drone when he speaks. Lucky for us, he's not too interested in other people and prefers the company of his books and immediate entourage.

The Dr. Jekyll and Mr. Hyde: This is the guy you have to meet to believe. In a matter of one conversation, he can mutate from one person to its antithesis, naturally contradicting himself and baffling those around him. Not good boyfriend material, unless you happen to like thrillers.

CANCER

The Pseudo-Macho: This is the sensitive Crab who tries to play the tough guy, especially when he's feeling particularly vulnerable or threatened—the kind of guy who uses big words or gestures to intimidate his opponents. Still a Crab, but one in disguise.

The Eccentric: This is the Cancer man who goes overboard in the imagination department. This trait, combined with a greater capriciousness than other Crabs, produces a very bizarre person, who can blend into the next type of Crab.

The Drifter: The Crab who has no roots and wants no roots. He's like the drunken sailor, drifting from one port to the next, with no particular itinerary. He loves the water, usually loves to drink, and lives most of the time in his very fertile mind. Obviously a poor candidate for lasting partnership, unless you happen to be a bit on the bohemian side yourself.

LEO

The Cool Cat: The solitary Lion who sits alone atop his hill, pretending to need no one. Of course, it's just a facade—he's probably nursing deep wounds from a long time ago. Not very popular and can be as cold as ice. Brrrrrr . . .

The Big Softie: The Lion who doesn't need top billing. (In fact, he can even be submissive to a strong girlfriend or wife.) He's so nice and generous, he usually gets taken advantage of, by everyone. Might be the perfect dad.

VIRGO

The Bad Boy: Believe it or not, there is a Virgo man who lost his virginity eons ago. This is the one who drinks, smokes, calls in sick to work, and regularly misses his doctor appointments. (And guess what, his pad's a mess, too.) This Virgo man is often quite social and loves to be where the action is. Probably the by-product of a formerly uptight lifestyle, and most likely not getting married anytime soon.

LIB RA

The Lady's Man: Here's the Libra man who can't keep his hands off beautiful women. He can be married and have ten children, but will go from one affair to the next. Not a bad person really, just too weak to resist.

The Snob: Yuck, this is the total snob; the man who sizes you up and turns his back if you don't meet his standards. Unlike other Libras, he's undiplomatic and doesn't feel the need to communicate to those beneath him. Huge social climber, too.

SCORPIO

Mr. Guy Next Door: This is the man who defies all Scorpio traits—there's nothing mysterious about him, he seems quite harmless, and he's actually a really nice guy. One of the more benign Scorpions, who probably never had to struggle with (or was even aware of) a darker nature. Must have had a great home life and lots of affection from Mom. Very safe to date.

Mr. Constipated: Oh, not one of the sexier Scorpions around. This is the man who's been holding it all in for decades—all his fears, defeats, frustrations—resulting in an overly uptight and rigid Scorpion, the kind that probably needs some really great sex soon. Still, he can be transformed by the right woman, and might even be worth the trouble.

SAGITTARIUS

The Lone Wolf: He doesn't look like a Sagittarius guy, that's for sure. Instead of outgoing and bubbly, he's withdrawn and a bit anti-social, preferring to explore on his own rather than with the group. Often very smart, but not patient enough to deal with other less-gifted mortals. Not great for relationships.

The Zeus: This is the Archer who feels more like a god than a man. Often feels above the law and can never be wrong. He might even believe he has special powers the rest of us are lacking. In any case, he can come off as a bit arrogant, but still ends up lucking out somehow.

The Reverse Snob: A strange phenomenon. This is the Sag man who pretends he couldn't care less for money (especially if he already has it). He'll go around in ripped jeans and berate us all for being too materialistic and greedy; but, at the same time, he'll sport an expensive watch and spend tons of money on costly trips or toys. A very difficult character to deal with, better left on his own.

CAPRICORN

The Grinch: Most Capricorn men are wise with money, but this one is amazingly cheap, the type who might reuse his brown paper lunch bags. He could be *loaded,* yet live like a penniless bum. He probably knows that Goats have a tendency to live until a very advanced age and is saving for the far future. Not fun company for Christmas.

The Outlaw: This is the Goat who scoffs at the rules, which he sees as made for others and not for him. In his quest for success or glory, he'll run over anyone and anything, without a second thought to the consequences, and has no respect for authority. Probably wouldn't be a pleasant life companion, so think twice if you bump into this one.

The Recluse: This is the Capricorn man who lives alone, often near the mountains or other not-too-populated areas. He usually withdraws from society out of disgust for humankind or life. Obviously, not someone you'll ever want to meet.

AQUARIUS

The Loner: This is the Aquarius man who always felt different and never managed to fit in or make friends. He'd probably be happy to meet a woman who could understand him and might be one of the only Aquarius men eager for an exclusive relationship.

The Rebel Without a Cause: Not the most fun guy to be around, he's always ranting about something, looking for trouble, or going against the rules (or authority), just for the sake of it. Probably trying to prove something, but what? Not someone you'd want to invest in.

The Star: This brand of Aquarius man has major charisma and can send a current of electricity through any room he enters. Of course, he's aware of his powerful effect on the rest of us and is even more difficult to pin down than the other Waterbearers out there.

PISCES

The Charlatan: Watch out for this one. Here's the Fish who can mutate into any shape he wants, at any time. He lives in a web of lies; comes into your life and disappears like that; could be a double-agent, a gypsy, or a thief. In any case, not reliable in the love department, or any other department, so don't even bother.

The Total Enigma: This Fish is a mystery to everyone. Just looking at him, you wonder what could possibly be going on in his head. He might be a genius, or a basket case; you'll probably never know and you'll probably want to pass on him, anyway.

The Megalomaniac: This is not a nice Fish at all. He's completely self-deluded, believes in his own grandiosity and personal omnipotence, and ends up alienating himself from everyone, even his family and friends. Usually the result of mental disorder or maybe even childhood suffering.

The Victim: This is the poor Fish—everybody's sucker—who is constantly victimized, probably because he's so gentle and can't say no. Or, he might play the martyr, ready to sacrifice his own happiness for the sake of others (especially if he finds something romantic about martyrdom). This person is often too good for this world and really deserves the love of a wonderful woman, one who can help him sort out the real friends from the users.

Just an Afterthought

You're probably wishing you read this book years before it was published so you could have figured out the men who got away *before* they got away (or before you sent them packing!). But if you're reading this now, you probably have your eye on a certain man out there, so good luck in bedazzling him. And I say *luck,* because information isn't everything. Sure, information is power, but even that is not enough when it comes to love. There're so many factors involved in a successful relationship—timing, chemistry, destiny—simply knowing a man and what he likes in a woman cannot guarantee that he will fall for her (if it were that easy, we could all hook Tom Cruise). But this knowledge can give you the best chance you've got.

And for those of you in despair about the supposed incompatibility between you and a potential boyfriend, don't take it *that* seriously. Sure, some people *usually* get along better with some rather than others, but any two people can form a winning couple if the alchemy is there. Look at Aquarius Ronald Reagan and Cancer Nancy Reagan—they obviously had a deep bond and a long-lasting marriage. And I rated the compatibility of an Aquarius man/Cancer woman couple as "challenging."

Just the same, there are lots of exceptions when it comes to the sun signs. Just because a Gemini man has the reputation to be something of a flirt doesn't mean he can't be loyal. In fact, a Gemini man can fall so in love that he can't *see* straight anymore! *Any* man who's really in love can be faithful, no matter what sun sign he was born under. So don't stress about some of the less pleasant aspects you read about—they don't necessarily apply to your guy. (Still, it never hurts to know the worst one can expect—at least that's my philosophy.)

Instead, focus on the positive aspects of the man you want (and be happy you can finally understand some of his strange behavior). Love has a better chance of blossoming in an auspicious climate, so *know your man* early on and give your best shot at making a lasting connection.

Acknowledgments

First, I want to thank the gang in New York for making this book happen! A huge thanks to Virgo coagent Laura Yorke, the first East Coaster to read the rough draft and urge me to continue. Her advice and support were invaluable (and it was fun comparing husband notes). Then, a great thanks to Sagittarius superagent Kim Witherspoon for taking on this project and using her know-how to sell it. Also, thanks to her assistants, Taurus Alexis Hurley and Scorpio Kerri Kolen *(au revoir et bonne chance),* for answering all my questions. Then, I couldn't have done it without my editor, Scorpio Jennifer Kasius, who was passionate about the material from the beginning and used her uncanny insight to shape the text into something we'd all want to read. Thank you, Jennifer! Also, thanks to Gemini Jim Coleman for knowing a million people and making the first crucial introduction that set this project rolling.

Of course, it wouldn't do to forget my girlfriends, all around the globe, who were a huge help (and some without even realizing it). I was pleased to hear my own suspicions confirmed over and over again, and I must admit I did learn a few things throughout the years (aren't "girls' nights" fun?). A special thanks to Virgo Maria Kling, who took the time to read my very first pages and encouraged me to continue. Maybe I needed her vote of confidence (and constructive criticism) before going in for the long haul. Anyway, I couldn't have done it without you, girlfriends, and I never would have had the idea in the first place if you didn't pester me all the time! Hope it was worth the wait.

A big thanks to my family, old and new, who supported me throughout the venture. And a special thanks to my curious Gemini sister-in-law, Kristi, who always showed extraordinary interest in my book idea and helped me to know I was doing something important. Then, I can't possibly forget my Cancer father, who thinks I share his writing bug and was always inquiring about the latest developments. (Hopefully he'll believe me when I tell him that research, the *hands-off* kind, provided me with the information to write about the intimate details of so many types of men. Cross my heart, Dad.) And, lastly, thanks to my sweet Libra husband, Michael, who was so patient this last year and gave me plenty of space to write.

Though she'll probably never read this, thank you to Lissandrine, the strange Pisces psychic lady in Marseilles who somehow "knew" I was writing a book for women and predicted it would be published. Guess what, Lissandrine? You were right!